m 4500
$7.50

THE GIRL SCOUTS AT PENGUIN PASS
or
TRAIL OF THE SNOWMAN

"Judy groped until she found the item."
THE GIRL SCOUTS AT PENGUIN PASS   *(See page 156)*

The GIRL SCOUTS at Penguin Pass

or
TRAIL OF THE SNOWMAN

by

Mildred A. Wirt

ILLUSTRATED

CUPPLES AND LEON COMPANY

Publishers   *New York*

Copyright, 1953, by
CUPPLES AND LEON COMPANY

———

ALL RIGHTS RESERVED

———

The Girl Scouts at Penguin Pass
or
Trail of the Snowman

Printed in the United States of America

CONTENTS

Chapter		Page
1	Tenderfoot Scout	1
2	"On My Honor"	2
3	A Bus Accident	21
4	Candy Mountain	29
5	Maple Leaf Lodge	39
6	A Night's Lodging	47
7	Mystery and Mice	55
8	Penguin Pass	61
9	A Snowman Guard	73
10	The Reluctant Caretaker	81
11	A Photograph Album	90
12	A Locked Stable	100
13	A Forbidden Trail	109
14	Retreat	117
15	A Severed Wire	129
16	Adventure	140
17	The Igloo Stonehouse	151
18	Into the Blizzard	159
19	Shelter	167
20	Another Loss	177
21	A Missing Item	184
22	Discovery	189
23	The Pursuit	195
24	Emergency Alarm	202
25	A Resignation	211

Chapter 1

Tenderfoot Scout

HARD, white, whirling flakes of snow blanketed Gypsy Hill. Lowering her face for protection against the stinging pellets, Judy Grant swooped down the ski run and christied to a fast stop almost at the door of the shelter house.

The long hill now was bleak and deserted, for the late afternoon had turned cold. Sharp, biting snow and wind had sent even the most hardy skiers to cover.

Judy, as usual, was the last to abandon a sport she dearly loved. Regretfully, she parked her hickory skis against the outer shelter house wall and opened the door into the warm, smoky building.

The big barren room seemed fairly filled with skiers who had taken refuge there to dry out mittens and toast numbed toes by the open fire. All were girls in their early teens, seated in a somewhat formal semi-circle.

"Hi," Judy greeted the group cheerfully. "Mind if I share your fire?"

"Glad to have you. Come on in." A red-haired girl in a green snowsuit made room for her near the hearth.

"I hope I'm not breaking up a meeting," Judy

said, with a ready smile. She had dark, wavy hair, warm brown eyes and a sprinkling of tiny freckles on the bridge of a pert little nose. "You're all Girl Scouts, aren't you?"

The question was friendly, rather than inquisitive. Judy liked people and naturally was a good mixer. Now a Freshman in Kirtland School, she was well advanced for her thirteen years, and an excellent athlete. As yet she was not very well acquainted in Fairfield, for the Grant family had moved there only recently.

"We're the Beaver Patrol—Intermediate Scouts. And we *were* having an informal meeting."

Judy's question had been answered curtly by Beverly Chester, an eighth grader with long, straight brown hair which swept somewhat untidily over the collar of her heavy jacket.

"Why, Beverly!" quietly reproved a young woman as she stirred the fire with a poker. Miss Louise Ward was leader of the Scout troop and a swimming teacher at Fairfield Y.W.C.A. "It really isn't a meeting, you know. Only an informal get-together."

"Besides, this is a public shelter house," added Kathleen Atwell, the girl in the green snowsuit. "Everyone is welcome, Judy Grant particularly so."

"You know my name!"

Kathleen nodded and smiled. "Everyone on Gypsy Hill does. You're such a fine skier."

"Oh, Goodness, no." Judy was rather embarrassed by the compliment. "And I do think I'm intruding at a private meeting."

"Please stay," urged Betty Bache, another Scout, who wore the well-tailored green uniform of the organization beneath her ski suit.

Virginia Cunningham and Ardeth Padgett, two other active patrol members, nodded quick assent. Only Beverly remained silently unfriendly to the invitation.

Kathleen introduced Judy to all the girls and then said: "We weren't having a regular business meeting. Our patrol merely was discussing an out-of-town ski trip we're planning next month."

"Better join the organization and come along," invited Ardeth, half-jokingly. She was a plump, good-natured girl, who preferred books to outdoor exercise. "The more the merrier, you know!"

"Wouldn't I love to go!" Judy replied, her brown eyes sparkling. "I've always wanted to be a Girl Scout. In the mid-western town where I spent most of my life, we had no troop."

"You mean you're really interested?" Kathleen asked quickly. "Why, Judy, we'd love to have you. Wouldn't we, girls?"

There was a chorus of assent. Again Beverly remained non-committal, an attitude which Judy immediately noted.

"I appreciate the invitation," she replied. "Truly I do. But I guess your patrol probably is filled—you have your own group—"

"Scouting is for any girl who is interested and will live up to the organization's laws," Miss Ward said. "Our patrol is small. So, if you care to join, Judy, we'd like to have you."

"Oh, I do want to belong!"

"There's quite a bit to it," Beverly Chester warned. "Even to become a Tenderfoot Scout one has to learn the Scout Promise, all the laws, the slogan, the motto, the history of the organization, and a lot of other useful things."

"Beverly, you make it sound frightfully hard," Miss Ward said. "It's really very easy."

"Two of the Scout Laws always seemed especially important to me," remarked Kathleen. She gazed pointedly at Beverly as she spoke. "One, *A Girl Scout is Courteous.*"

"That's the fifth law on the list," Ardeth contributed. "Altogether, there are ten."

"The other law I had in mind is the fourth one," Kathleen went on. "*A Girl Scout is a friend to all and a sister to every other Girl Scout.*"

The deep flush which overspread Beverly's face did not come from the warmth of the fire.

"I didn't intend to make it sound hard," she mumbled. "I only thought Judy should understand what she's up against. Besides, if she's joining in the

Tenderfoot Scout

expectation of making the trip with us, it's rather hopeless. She couldn't possibly become a Girl Scout and learn everything in time—"

"Why not?" interposed Miss Ward. "If Judy has a quick memory and a will to work, she can complete the requirements and be invested after four sessions."

"Could you make every meeting?" Kathleen asked encouragingly. "You wouldn't dare skip even one, because our outing is in exactly a month."

"I think I can do it," Judy replied with quiet confidence. "Besides the Laws, what else must I learn?"

"The Scout Motto," Virginia informed her. "But that's easy. It's 'Be Prepared.'"

"Our slogan isn't hard either, though sometimes it's difficult to put it into practice," contributed Betty Bache. "'Do a Good Turn Daily.'"

"We'll all help you with the laws and the Promise," Ardeth offered.

Miss Ward told Judy that she also would be expected to know how the flag of the U.S.A. should be displayed. Another requirement, she explained, was the choice of an activity from categories designated as "Homemaking" and "Out of Doors" and the proof by achievement in these fields that she understood the Scout laws.

"I'm not too good at housework."

"Oh, that requirement is easy," Betty declared.

"To pass it, you can set a table at home at least once a day for a week, or make your own bed for the same length of time."

"The out-of-doors requirements are simple too," encouraged Kathleen. "You can make a rough sketch map of the route you follow from home to school or to our troop meeting place. You mark on the traffic lights, crossings, and other hazards. Or you could demonstrate that you know how to use a compass."

"I'll select that last requirement," Judy decided quickly. "My brother Ted has a good compass, and sometimes he lets me use it."

"You're the same as a Tenderfoot Scout, right now," Kathleen declared, well pleased. "Just don't miss any meetings. Our next one is tomorrow night at Scout headquarters."

"I know the building," Judy nodded. "Thanks for wanting me."

Betty gathered up her mittens and began to button her heavy jacket.

"It's getting late," she announced. "I have to run."

"So do I," added Virginia, reluctantly pulling herself away from the fire. "Goodbye, Judy. We'll see you tomorrow at seven sharp."

One by one, the girls began to leave. Judy too abandoned the shelter, walking outside with Kathleen. Snow still was falling.

"Judy, we're awfully glad to have you as a member, Kathleen said sincerely. "Don't mind Beverly. She means well, but at times she's a bit snippy."

"What she said didn't bother me."

"I'm glad of that. Beverly is our patrol leader. We chose her rather on the spur-of-the-moment, I'm afraid. When she first joined, her parents had the entire troop up to the Chester Lodge on Lake Tabor. We had a wonderful time, and were sort of carried away, I guess. Anyway, we chose Beverly for patrol leader, without giving enough thought to the basic requirements for the job. She means well though."

"I know," Judy smiled as she slung her skis over her shoulder. "Beverly is the type who speaks her mind. She didn't like the way I barged in, and I can't blame her. Furthermore, she thinks I'm joining Beaver Patrol because I want to go on the skiing trip."

"If you can go, it will be a break for us. Maybe you can teach us a trick or two in skiing. You do it so beautifully."

"I've practiced a lot, Kathleen. I'll be glad to help the girls if I can. By the way, where is the patrol going?"

"To Candy Mountain."

"That's nearly a day's drive from here."

"We'll go by bus," Kathleen explained. "I've heard the skiing is grand there. Miss Ward is arrang-

The Girl Scouts at Penguin Pass

ing for us to stay a full week at Maple Leaf Lodge. We'll go during Christmas vacation."

"Maple Leaf Lodge?" A startled expression flickered across Judy's freckled face. Her brown eyes widened in obvious surprise.

"Yes, the Boy Scout Lodge. It's closed this winter. But an old caretaker is there the year-around and Miss Ward thinks she can arrange for us to have the lodge an entire week."

"I-I didn't know you were going to Maple Leaf Lodge."

The two girls now were trudging toward the bus stop, weighted down by their equipment. Kathleen turned to glance curiously at her new friend. Even in the blinding, driving snow she could see Judy's lips drawn into a tight, almost grim line.

"You don't seem very well pleased about it, Judy," she commented. "Anything wrong with Maple Leaf Lodge?"

"Why, no. Not the lodge."

"Candy Mountain then?"

"I've heard the skiing is excellent there."

"Well, something is wrong," Kathleen said flatly. "You don't much like the idea of going to the Boy Scout lodge, do you?"

"It's none of my affair, Kathleen. I'm not even a full-fledged Tenderfoot Scout yet."

"But you do have an opinion."

Tenderfoot Scout

"My brother, Ted is a Boy Scout," Judy explained reluctantly. "He's away now at a private school. But earlier this winter, he spent a week at the lodge."

"I take it he didn't write such glowing reports."

"It's not that, Kathleen."

"Then what is wrong, Judy? If you know anything unfavorable about Maple Leaf Lodge, it's your duty to tell me."

The girls had paused at the bus stop. Judy rested her long skis on the street curb.

"I don't want to spoil the fun," she said slowly. "I don't really KNOW anything. It's just that Ted wrote—"

"Yes, go on," Kathleen urged impatiently.

"He didn't write anything against Maple Leaf Lodge. But he did say something rather alarming about Candy Mountain, or rather Penguin Pass."

"The risk of snow slides?"

"No, his letter was vague. He mentioned Penguin Pass, not far from the lodge, hinting of a mystery and danger. He said the scoutmaster seemed quite relieved when the troop was enroute home."

"What sort of danger and mystery, Judy?"

"I haven't the slightest idea. I wouldn't have said anything about it, only you dragged it from me, Kathleen,"

"Miss Ward should know." Kathleen's well-shaped

eyebrows arched into a troubled pucker. "But if we tell her what you've just told me, the trip to Candy Mountain may be called off."

"And possibly for a trivial reason," Judy added. "Ted is inclined to exaggerate sometimes. It may not mean anything. Then again—"

Kathleen spoke decisively. "A Girl Scout isn't supposed to guess or take chances. There's only one thing to do. Write your brother right away, and ask for complete information."

"I'll do it."

"Another thing," Kathleen warned hurriedly, for her bus now was approaching. "Not a word of this to the other girls until we know the real situation. No use alarming them unnecessarily."

"I'll get as much information as I can," Judy promised. With a quick laugh, she added: "Even a Tenderfoot, you know, believes in being prepared!"

Chapter 2

"On My Honor"

SOFT flakes of snow banked the windows of Scout Headquarters, but inside the great hall, there was warmth and friendliness. The all-important hour of Judy Grant's investiture into the Beaver Patrol was at hand.

For weeks, the determined girl had worked and studied, preparing herself for this moment when she must be examined upon her knowledge.

"All set, Judy?" Kathleen asked as the two friends stood together in the corridor.

"I think so." Judy spoke with quiet confidence.

"Good! You'll pass with flying colors, I know. And it will be wonderful having you with us at Maple Leaf Lodge. By the way, did you hear anything more from your brother about—you know."

Judy had no chance to answer, for just then Miss Ward opened the door to say that the ceremony would begin. Kathleen squeezed her friend's hand encouragingly, and they entered the hall together.

The entire troop stood in horseshoe formation, facing the American flag. Everyone except Judy wore the neat, dark green tailored Girl Scout uniform with belt of green webbing, low-heeled shoes and green anklets marked with the organization insignia.

The entire troop pledged allegiance to the flag and sang "America." Then as the Scouts stood straight and proud in an impressive formation, Kathleen led Judy forward, introducing her formally to Miss Ward and the group.

"We are happy to have you join our organization," Miss Ward told Judy. "You have worked very hard these last few weeks. Are you ready now to make your Promise?"

"I am," Judy replied earnestly. Slowly and thoughtfully, she repeated the words:

"'On my honor, I will try:
To do my duty to God and my country,
To help other people at all times,
To obey the Girl Scout Laws.'"

"Well spoken, Judy!" Miss Ward approved. "You have now taken upon yourself a code of honor by which you must live, not occasionally, but every day of your life. You must think first of other people, not yourself. You may find that it is not always easy to live up to the Promise, but you must make a sincere effort."

"I'll try," Judy said. "I'll try hard, because more than anything else I want to be a Girl Scout."

"And we want you, Judy. I'm sure you will be a credit to Beaver Patrol." Miss Ward then pinned a trefoil pin on the left side of the girl's dark dress, a symbol that she was at last, a Tenderfoot Scout.

All the girls repeated the ten laws of the organiza-

"On My Honor"

tion, which brought the ceremony to a close. One by one, the Scouts came to shake Judy's hand and to tell her they were glad she would be able to make the trip with them to Candy Mountain.

"You certainly slid in under the wire," Beverly remarked. "We leave tomorrow at 10 a.m. Be sure to have your luggage at the bus station at least fifteen minutes early."

"I'll be there," Judy promised.

"Remember, only one bag, your bed roll and skiing equipment," Miss Ward warned the group. "Bring only sensible clothing, for the weather may be very cold at Maple Leaf Lodge. You all have a suggested list of items."

"I hope the weather gives us a break," remarked Ardeth, glancing dubiously at the snow-banked windows. "How long will the bus trip take, Miss Ward?"

"About six hours. I've made all arrangements with Mr. Medford, the Scout leader, for use of the lodge. The caretaker, Caleb Shively, will meet us at Weston to drive us up the mountain."

"Judy, it would be nicer if you could get your Scout uniform before we leave," Betty Bache remarked. "It's not necessary, of course."

"I'll dash down to the department store, first thing in the morning," Judy promised. "I want to buy a Scout compass too and some other equipment."

"Tenderfoot, with your new compass, we'll depend upon you to prevent the patrol from getting lost at Penguin Pass," Beverly said. She laughed as she made the remark, yet her words had a tiny sharp edge which jarred slightly upon the group.

To cover an awkward silence, Kathleen seized Judy's hand, leading her away to see a nature exhibit the patrol had completed that week.

"Don't pay a bit of attention to Beverly," she whispered. "Down under, she's very good hearted. It's just that she says things without thinking—"

"It didn't bother me a bit," Judy said lightly. "Anyway, a compass is a useful item to have on a mountain. And from what I've heard about Penguin Pass—"

"Just what *have* you heard, Judy?"

The question was asked, not by Kathleen, but by Beverly, who had come up quietly from behind.

"I've heard that the mountain is a rugged one," Judy answered. "Some of the trials are steep and treacherous."

"Miss Ward wouldn't take us there to ski if it weren't safe," Beverly said in a manner intended to set a Tenderfoot once and for all in her place. "I shouldn't worry about it, if I were you."

"I'm not worrying," Judy answered. She gave no hint of annoyance. "Well, see you at the bus station! I must hurry home now, because I have a million things to do before we leave tomorrow. 'Bye!"

"On My Honor"

The following morning dawned cold and cloudy. Judy pulled herself out of bed at six o'clock to pack her single bag with lightweight but warm woolen garments she would need at Maple Leaf Lodge.

"I'll drop your luggage off for you at the bus station," her father offered at the breakfast table. "Also your skis and poles."

"Thanks, Dad," Judy said gratefully. "That will save me carrying them. I want to do an errand at the department store and it doesn't open until nine o'clock. That won't give me much time."

"Don't miss the bus just to buy yourself a Scout uniform," her mother advised.

"I won't," Judy laughed. "Never fear! I'll be on that bus when it pulls out. Nothing could keep me from Candy Mountain!"

Efficiently, the girl made a last check of her belongings before turning over the suitcase, bed roll and skiing equipment to her father.

By nature, she was orderly, and early in grade school had acquired the knack of "thinking ahead." From her brother, Ted, she had learned all outdoor sports, and also from him had picked up good sportsmanship. Judy was striking in appearance with shiny black, well-brushed hair, but could not be classified as "pretty." She had charm though, and an alert mind which made school easy for her.

Judy was waiting at the department store five minutes before the doors opened. Shivering in the chilly vestibule, she scanned the cloudy sky with misgiving.

"Looks as if another snow might be on the way," she thought. "Or possibly sleet. I hope not, because bad weather might delay our bus."

The store doors presently opened, and Judy made a dash for the Girl Scout department on the third floor. Quickly she tried on and bought a neat fitting uniform, a Scout knife, a compass and a canteen. With the package under her arm, she then hastened toward the bus station.

As she crossed the street, a strong gust of wind nearly bowled her over. She clutched her package, and then saw a hat go rolling down the street ahead of her.

The headgear had been lost by an elderly lady, who uttered a cry of dismay as she watched it cartwheel along the curb.

Glancing both ways to make certain no car was bearing down, Judy pursued and finally captured the runaway hat.

"Thank you, my dear," the woman murmured gratefully as she returned it. "This wind is so strong! I scarcely can walk into it."

"Let me help you," Judy offered, taking her arm.

The old lady walked very slowly. As they passed a clock in a jewelry store window, Judy noted with some alarm that it was now ten minutes before 10 o'clock. And the bus was scheduled to leave sharp on the hour.

"I can make it alone now," the old lady said just then. "Thank you, my dear, for being so kind."

"Are you certain you'll be all right?"

"Yes, indeed. I have less than a half block to go."

Eager to be away, Judy hastened on with her package. Fearful of being late, she ran the last block.

Breathless and winded, she reached the bus station at five minutes to ten. However, as she swung in through the entrance doors, she saw the big bus standing in the garage ready to depart.

The group of Scouts, Kathleen, Beverly, Betty, Virginia and Ardeth stood hemmed in by luggage, anxiously watching the entranceway.

"Here she comes!" Beverly exclaimed. "Just in time too!"

"I'm sorry to be late," Judy apologized breathlessly. "I—I was delayed."

Beverly had noted with disapproval the parcel under the girl's arm. "We were supposed to bring only one bag," she said pointedly. "Bundles make so much muss and clutter."

"I didn't want to go without a Scout uniform," Judy replied. By this time she had located the suitcase which her father had delivered for her. Quickly opening it, she popped the bundle inside. "There!" she declared cheerfully. "How's that? No muss. No fuss. No clutter."

"Okay, Tenderfoot," Beverly returned. "Let's get aboard now, before all the seats are gone."

The girls seated themselves at the rear of the bus. Kathleen slid in beside Judy; Beverly sat with Miss Ward, and the others arranged themselves directly behind.

The bus was late in starting. Finally, a young man with a cheerful grin, squeezed into the drver's seat. He checked his passengers and the bus moved out of the station.

Only then did the girls notice with some misgiving that a cold rain had started to fall. With the temperature just below freezing, the drops froze as fast as they struck the pavement.

"Ice," said Beverly grimly. "Now we'll have a long slow trip to Weston."

"I'm afraid we'll never make it in six hours," Miss Ward agreed.

"We have a good driver though," Betty Bache noted cheerfully.

The bus threaded it sway through Fairfield and soon was moving smoothly along the country highway. The road was clear of snow, and it was only on the occasional stops for lights that the vehicle tended to skid a bit.

For the first two hours of the ride, the girls chatted, but the purr of the motor gradually lulled them into a semi-drowsy state. Judy and Kathleen relaxed completely, dozing off. They awoke re-

"On My Honor"

freshed, to note that the rain had ceased. Roads however, remained slippery and there were deeper banks of snow along the ditches.

"Where are we now?" Kathleen inquired. "Almost there?"

"Almost there, my eye!" Virginia chuckled. "We're not even half way, and making poor time."

The bus presently halted for lunch. The girls stretched their legs, freshened up in the cafe washroom and then had sandwiches and hot chocolate.

"All right, folks," the bus driver urged his passengers along. "Everyone aboard. We're running late."

The Scouts obeyed promptly. Other passengers were slower to follow instructions. Finally though, the bus again was on its way.

Presently, great flakes of damp snow began to whirl against the windows of the vehicle. They banked up on the panes which frosted over so that less and less of the highways and fields was visible.

"My, wouldn't you hate to drive a bus on a day such as this—" Kathleen began.

Her words ended in a little scream, for suddenly the bus driver swerved the steering wheel and put on the brakes hard. So unexpected was the movement, that passengers lurched sideways in their seats.

A car shot across the road, directly in the path of the bus. Only by quick thinking and skill did the bus driver avoid a collision.

But the danger was not past. The sudden braking of the massive vehicle on the icy road had thrown it into a skid. Losing traction, it went into a long terrifying slide, heading for a deep ditch at the right hand side of the road.

Chapter 3

A Bus Accident

THE sandy-haired driver fought desperately to recover control of the skidding bus. He could not, and with a hard jolt the carrier slid into the deep ditch.

Judy and Kathleen were flung violently forward in their seat. Across the aisle, Beverly, caught off guard, was hurled onto the floor. The other Scouts and Miss Ward managed to retain their places, though they were considerably jarred.

The bus hung over the ditch, tilted far on its side. Several women passengers, more frightened than hurt, began to scream. A few tried to push their way toward the exits.

"Everyone keep his seat!" the bus driver shouted. "There is no danger. I will open the doors."

Judy pulled Beverly to her feet. The patrol leader had not been hurt. She was annoyed though to have sprawled so awkwardly on the floor.

"Of all the stupid drivers!" she muttered. "This one takes the prize!"

"It wasn't his fault," Judy replied, helping Beverly into her seat. "He had to swerve to avoid hitting a car. This could have been a lot worse."

By this time, the bus driver had opened a rear emergency door. One by one the Girl Scouts scrambled out into the biting winter air and helped other passengers up the slippery incline to the pavement.

Only one woman had been injured by the jolt. Her left arm had been bruised, though not seriously so.

While the driver tried to move the big bus out of the ditch, Miss Ward and Kathleen improvised a sling from a neck scarf. It served the woman very well, easing the arm pain.

After several attempts to get the bus out of the ditch under its own power, the driver gave it up.

"No use, folks," he announced. "We'll have to be pulled out."

"And what are we to do meanwhile?" a nervous passenger demanded. "Stand here and freeze to death? I have two small children."

"If you want to stay inside the bus, I can keep the motor running for warmth," the driver said. "I suggest though, that you all wait at the next town of Fayetteville. It's less than a quarter of a mile down the road. There's a good cafe—Miller's. It may take awhile to get this bus on the road again."

Most of the passengers accepted the situation goodnaturedly. A few, however, grumbled at the delay and inconvenience.

The bus driver hailed a passing motorist. He arranged for the injured woman to be taken to a doctor at Fayetteville, and for assistance to be sent

A Bus Accident

from the nearest garage. Other automobiles came by, picking up groups of passengers.

Judy and Kathleen were among the last to reach Miller's Cafe. The little restaurant was fairly jammed with disgruntled passengers, all demanding hot coffee and food. Quite overwhelmed by such rush business, the one waitress fluttered about, trying to serve everyone at once.

One passenger, in particular, was very unreasonable. He was a tall, dark-eyed man in a brown suit and derby hat. Judy recalled that he had boarded the bus some distance from Fairfield and had sat alone.

"Come on, girlie," he beckoned to the harassed waitress. "Get a move on, can't you? I've waited fifteen minutes now for my coffee."

"Sorry, sir," the girl replied. "I'm waiting on folks as fast as I can. The coffee's run out and we're making more."

The Girl Scouts waited until all the other passengers had been served before asking for any attention. Their consideration was appreciated by the waitress, who said:

"I wish everyone would take it easy, as the Scouts do. A body only has two hands!"

The Girl Scouts deeply regretted the delay which would make them very late in reaching Weston. Nevertheless, they kept their disappointment to themselves. To pass the time and to cheer the other passengers, they sang songs in which all were invited to join. Time passed rather quickly.

Judy therefore, was rather startled when she saw by the clock that two full hours had slipped away.

"My! We will be late reaching Weston!" she exclaimed. "I only hope Caleb Shively doesn't get tired waiting for us."

The brown-suited stranger, sipping his fourth cup of black coffee glanced intently at the girl. Hitherto he had ignored all the Scouts, taking no part in their songs.

"So you're going to Weston?" he inquired.

"We are if this bus of ours ever comes," Judy replied. "Our patrol plans to ski at Maple Leaf Lodge."

Again the stranger eyed her intently. "That the Boy Scouts place?" he demanded.

"Why, yes, it is. Are you by chance going to Weston also?"

The man did not answer. Whether or not he had heard the question, Judy could not know. At any rate, he turned his back, and paying her no further attention, went on sipping coffee.

"He's a queer one," Kathleen whispered a moment later. "The depressing type."

To the relief of everyone, the bus rolled up to the cafe door twenty minutes later. None the worse for its mis-adventure, the carrier now was reserviced and ready to continue its journey.

A Bus Accident

As the Girl Scouts climbed aboard, Miss Ward asked the driver what time they might expect to reach Weston.

"Hard to say," he replied. "We're more than three hours late now and the roads are icy. We may make it by seven or eight o'clock. No earlier, I'm afraid."

"This trip certainly isn't starting out well," Kathleen remarked as she seated herself beside Judy again. "Trouble! Trouble!"

"And we may run into more of it when we get there," Judy hinted.

"Meaning?"

"Oh, nothing."

"You had something in mind, Judy. Were you thinking about Penguin Pass and that letter your brother wrote?"

"Maybe. I shouldn't have said it, Kathy. That remark sort of slipped out."

"Judy," Kathleen said soberly, "you never told me what your brother wrote. The second time, I mean. What did he tell you about Penguin Pass?"

"Nothing good."

"Please, Judy, you shouldn't keep it to yourself."

"Ted advised me not to make the trip, Kathy."

"You never said a word about it at any of our meetings!"

"The letter came only three days ago. Ted hates to write and he's slow answering. Anyway, I have nothing definite to report. He wrote again that he didn't consider the locality safe because of something that happened there—"

"Say, what are you girls talking so soberly about?" Beverly broke in curiously from across the aisle. "Scouts shouldn't have secrets from one another."

"We were speaking of Judy's brother," Kathleen replied.

The answer seemed to satisfy Beverly, for she subsided into silence.

Kathleen and Judy did not resume their discussion. They purposely avoided mention of Penguin Pass, feeling that it would be a mistake to alarm the other Scouts even by a hint that anything might be amiss at Maple Leaf Lodge.

The highway, which had swung through rolling foothills, soon became much steeper. Towns were farther apart. The terrain grew more rugged, and at times the bus labored to make the grades.

From the frosted window, the girls could see snowy pines peppering the slopes. As they wound deeper and deeper into the mountainous area, long shadows darkened the highway.

"It will be dark before we reach Weston," Kathleen remarked anxiously. "What a relief it will be to get settled at the lodge!"

Though the Scouts did not complain, they were now very tired. The trip had been an exhausting one, and the accident, although minor, had contributed to their discomfort and weariness. They longed

A Bus Accident

for a hot meal, comfortable beds, and a chance to sleep undisturbed.

Many of the passengers had left the bus by this time. Judy noted, however, that the man in the dark brown suit remained aboard. Apparently his destination was Weston, or beyond.

When it seemed to the girls that the journey never would come to an end, the bus swung into a little village nestled at the foot of Candy Mountain.

"Weston!" the driver called.

As the girls gathered their luggage, he told them that it had been a pleasure to have them aboard.

The bus pulled away, and the little group of Scouts was left standing beside the highway. Shivering, the girls looked up and down the dark, nearly deserted street.

Caleb Shively was nowhere in evidence, nor was there anyone to meet them. The only visible person was the strange passenger, who had alighted, and now was walking rapidly away.

Miss Ward noticed a lighted grocery store across the street. Determinedly, she herded her charges in that direction.

"What a situation!" Beverly muttered.. "After hours on the road, no one here to meet us."

"We couldn't expect Mr. Shively to stand and wait for hours," Ardeth declared. "He's probably taken refuge in a comfortable spot."

"Or at least left word for us," Betty added.

"Everything's fine now that we're here."

Loaded down by their skiis, bed rolls and suitcases, the girls crossed the road to the grocery store. Single file, they stomped in out of the snow to drop their belongings by the pot-bellied stove which blasted the room with heat.

"Well, well, WELL!" cackled the old store keeper, astonished by the influx of youthful visitors.

He was a stubby, spry man in his late 50's, with a pencil behind one ear and a white canvas apron covering a red plaid shirt.

"We're looking for Caleb Shively," Miss Ward said. "He was supposed to meet our bus, but it was hours late. Now we don't know where to find him."

The old store keeper came from behind the counter, eyeing the girls curiously.

"Now if that ain't too bad," he remarked.

"You mean Mr. Shively didn't wait for us?" Miss Ward inquired.

"He didn't wait, 'cause so far as I know, he never came," the old store keeper said. "The truth is, I ain't see that old caretaker for nigh onto two months."

Chapter 4

Candy Mountain

THE old store keeper's words came as the final discouragement of the day to the group of Girl Scouts. For a moment, no one spoke. Then Miss Ward said in a weak, thin voice:

"You say you haven't seen Mr. Shively in two months?"

"Yep, that's right."

"But he was expecting us. He was to have met us here hours ago. Perhaps he came to Weston earlier and tired of waiting for the bus."

The storekeeper, whose name was Jacob Hawkins, emptied a scuttle of coal into the stove before he replied.

"Caleb Shively ain't been in Weston today, or fer weeks," he said with finality. "You folks was planning on doing some skiing on the mountains, I take it?"

"Yes, we've engaged Maple Leaf Lodge for a week. We must go there tonight. Our bus was in an accident which delayed us. Now the girls are tired and hungry. The day has been a hard one."

Mr. Hawkins made a sympathetic clucking sound.

"Shoo now, that's too bad," he said. "I reckon you're jest out of luck."

"But why isn't Mr. Shively here to meet us?" Miss Ward asked in some exasperation. "If he didn't intend to come, he at least might have sent word."

"The roads are bad, and Old Caleb don't leave his comfortable fire if he can help it," the storeman returned. "He says the Boy Scouts lead him such a merry chase all summer, he has to hibernate all winter to catch up on his rest."

Miss Ward and the girls did not appreciate Mr. Hawkins' little joke. Their patience had been tried to the breaking point. In fact, it was all Virginia could do to prevent a tear from trickling down her cheeks. To keep the others from noticing, she pretended to study a row of glass jars on the store shelf.

"There's been some mix up," Miss Ward went on, a bit grimly. "Can we telephone the lodge from here?"

"Sure thing, go right ahead," Mr. Hawkins consented. " Phone's at the rear of the store. Two long rings and three short. I doubt if you can raise Caleb though. He ain't much on answering his phone."

While the girls clustered about, Miss Ward used the old fashioned telephone attached to the wall. Five times in succession she made the ring. But as Mr. Hawkins had predicted, there was no anwer.

"Line could be out of order," the storeman remarked. "I doubt it though. Caleb just ain't a mind to answer."

Until this moment, the Scouts had kept up their spirits fairly well. But now, it seemed to them that their anticipated outing was doomed to complete failure.

"Well, if this isn't a mess!" Beverly muttered in disgust. "I guess we might just as well go back to Fairfield!"

"Oh, don't be a sourpuss," Ardeth scolded her goodnaturedly. "This is just one of those things. It wasn't Miss Ward's fault that things went wrong. Take a cheerful view, Beverly."

"I'm sure we'd all feel peppier if we had something to eat," Judy remarked. "Is there a cafe near here, Mr. Hawkins?"

"Sure thing. Directly across the street. Ma's kitchen, they call it. Best food in Weston."

"Ma's Kitchen, here I come!" declared Kathleen, starting toward the door.

"Hold on," Mr. Hawkins stopped her. "The place ain't open. Closes at seven."

A moan of anguish from the Girl Scouts greeted this latest bit of bad news.

"Is there a hotel?" Miss Ward inquired, almost desperately. "Any place at all where we can get warm food and clean beds?"

"Nearest place is the Berkshire Arms, but that's half a mile up the mountain. Rates are a mite steep too. Three dollars a meal, not countin' tips."

"Jolly! Just jolly!" Beverly muttered. "I brought

exactly seven dollars with me for spending money."

"We'll have to reach Maple Leaf Lodge somehow," Miss Ward declared. "We have our reservations, paid for in advance. Is there a taxi service in the town?"

"Clem Davis runs a car."

"Then we'll employ him to take us to the lodge," Miss Ward said, greatly relieved. "How do I reach him?"

"You can't fer awhile," Mr. Hawkins said. "Five minutes ago I seen him drive past, headin' out of town with a passenger. Some man that got off the bus."

Miss Ward, now at her wit's end, sank down in a rocker beside the stove. "I—I don't know what to do," she confessed miserably. It's all my fault. I brought the girls here for a pleasant week of skiing —and now this."

"Shoo, no call to git discouraged, Miss," Mr. Hawkins said cheerfully.

"Perhaps you could suggest a way out of our predicament, Mr. Hawkins," Judy said, flashing her most friendly smile.

"Since you put it so nice-like, maybe I could," he grinned. "First off, if you ain't too particular, I can fix you up with a snack to eat."

"Particular!" Betty Bache exclaimed. "I could devour wall paper and relish it!"

"I can give you cheese, crackers, cookies, and

mugs of hot soup," the storekeeper offered. "Your choice of fruit—bananas, apples or oranges."

"Oh, that's splendid," Miss Ward approved. "We do appreciate your kindness."

"Glad to help you out," Mr. Hawkins said gruffly. "When you first breezed in off the bus, I thought maybe you were uppity city folks. Some of 'em give me a pain!"

The old store keeper bustled about, putting a kettle of tomato soup on the stove to heat. Judy and Kathleen helped him set out paper plates laden with other items gleaned from the shelves.

"Isn't there any way we can reach Maple Leaf Lodge tonight?" Judy asked as she opened a box of potato chips to serve with the soup. "Couldn't we hike up the mountain?"

"Tain't safe at night," Mr. Hawkins answered. "Besides, it's starting to snow again. Comin' down hot an' heavy."

"I'll try the lodge again," Miss Ward said wearily. "Perhaps this time Mr. Shively will answer."

As before, her repeated rings went unanswered.

"Now don't take it so hard, Miss," Mr. Hawkins chuckled when she returned to the group clustered about the stove. "I'll see that you reach Maple Lodge tonight, if you're set on going there."

"You will?" the Scout leader questioned eagerly.

"I'll hitch up my bob sled and haul you up the mountain," the store keeper promised. "Reckon I might as well shut up shop any time now. With this snow comin' down, the quicker we get started the better."

"You've saved the day for us!" Miss Ward exclaimed gratefully. "I'll pay you for your trouble, Mr. Hawkins."

"You won't pay me a penny," he fired back at her. "I'm just doing my good deed fer the day, that's all. Guess I know a little about Scouting myself," he added, winking at Judy.

While the girls finished their meal, the storekeeper went to hitch up his team. Before he returned, they had ample time to burn the paper plates and sweep away fallen crumbs.

Mr. Hawkins presently drew up in front of the store. He urged the girls into their snowsuits, remarking that the storm was increasing in intensity, and he was eager to be away.

The sky was filled with feathery plumes as the girls climbed into the bob-sled. Already the two big gray horses were covered with white and their breath made clouds of steam in the cold, night air.

"Snuggle down in the blankets," Mr. Hawkins advised, picking up the reins. "Wind's mighty sharp and the mercury's nosin' zero."

Well-fed and cheerful once more, the Scouts huddled together on the floor of the sled. Mr. Hawkins clucked to the horses and they glided smoothly away.

Candy Mountain

Despite the early hour, scarcely a light showed in the little village. At the edge of Weston, Mr. Hawkins turned right onto a narrow, winding road which spiraled up the mountain.

Blinded by the falling snow, the girls kept their faces under the blankets. Now and then, when they peeped out, they caught fleeting glimpses of snow-caked evergreens standing majestically on the steep slopes. The night was very dark.

"What do you suppose prevented Mr. Shively from meeting us?" Miss Ward asked the storeman. Though she sat at the front of the bob-sled, she had to shout to make herself heard above the whistle of the wind.

"No tellin'," Mr. Hawkins returned, touching his whip to one of the grays. "Matter o' fact, I'm a mite worried something may have happened."

"You think he might be ill?"

"Could be," Mr. Hawkins returned, turning his head to make himself heard. "Only thing is, his orders have been comin' through fer supplies. Only last week he ordered a box of staples sent out. He's been lettin' his bill run though, an' that ain't like Caleb."

The storekeeper's remarks threw an uneasy pall upon the girls. What might they expect at Maple Leaf Lodge? If the caretaker were ill or had not been expecting them, the planned outing might prove a miserable undertaking.

"I'm cold," Beverly shivered, pulling the blanket closer about her. "I wish we hadn't come."

"You should have worn warmer clothing," Virginia advised her.

Beverly's snowsuit had been chosen for appearance and though it was stylish and well-cut, she nearly always suffered from the cold. Pride would not permit her to wear a sweater beneath the jacket.

"We should be at the lodge soon," Judy said to encourage her. "Then we'll have a warm fire, nice beds and everything will seem fine."

"You hope," Beverly retorted. She burrowed deeper down into her collar, lapsing into gloomy silence.

The road rapidly became steeper, twisting through dense stands of forest. At intervals Mr. Hawkins stopped the horses to let them rest after an especially hard pull. On the down grades the sled went at a fast clip, its runners throwing up ice and snow.

Then abruptly, just as the girls were thoroughly adjusted to the bumps and dips of the road, the big sled came to a sudden halt.

"Are we there?" demanded Ardeth, lifting her head from beneath the blanket.

One by one, the girls raised up to peer at the dense wall of evergreens on either side of the road. There was no sign of a lodge or any other building.

"Sorry, girls," Mr. Hawkins called cheerily. "This is as far as I can take you. Everyone pile out!"

Beverly uttered a wail of dismay. "Why, this is the middle of the forest!" she protested.

"I'd take you to the lodge if I could," Mr. Hawkins said regretfully. "But the main road doesn't go that far. A private one leads on to Maple Leaf. Not a car nor a sled has been through this winter. Snows are drifted high. Reckon that's why Old Caleb ain't been to town lately."

"How far is the lodge?" Ardeth asked in a faint voice.

"Not far. Eighth of a mile maybe. Or less. You can't miss it from here."

"We have our luggage to carry, and skis," Beverly began, only to break off as she realized that she was voicing a complaint.

Following Judy's example, she leaped nimbly out of the sled and began to help unload equipment.

"Just follow the road and you can't miss the lodge," Mr. Hawkins advised. "I can let you have my lantern if you want it."

"We have our flashlights," Miss Ward replied. "From here we can make it all right. I—I just hope nothing is amiss at the lodge. It seems so strange Mr. Shively didn't meet us. I made arrangements weeks ago."

"You'll find him there all right," the storekeeper said, handing down the last piece of luggage. "Leastwise, his order for groceries came through last week. I always leave his stuff there by the fence. I see he's picked it up."

"We'll be all right," Miss Ward declared, hiding her nervousness. "Many thanks for bringing us this far."

"You're welcome, Miss," he replied, tipping his cap. "Well, goodnight to you all. Pleasant skiing!"

Mr. Hawkins turned his team around, and with a wave of his mittened hand, glided off down the mountain.

Left alone in the dark, the girls clustered together, tense and uncertain. The beams of their flashlights revealed a narrow, private road hemmed in with tall pines. Huge drifts alternated with patches of earth swept completely bare of snow.

A hush had fallen upon the group.

"Pleasant skiing," Beverly echoed hollowly. "Pleasant skiing!"

Shouldering her skis, Judy reached for her suitcase and bed roll.

"Come on, girls," she said resolutely, leading the way. "Better go easy on those flashlights though, because there's no telling how long we may need them."

Chapter 5

Maple Leaf Lodge

SINGLE file, the girls trudged wearily up the drifted road which seemed without end. There was less wind now in the shelter of the tall evergreens, but the intense cold of the night numbed their fingers and nipped their cheeks.

The snow itself provided some illumination, so unless the footing was uncertain, the Scouts conserved their flashlight batteries.

Burdened by heavy equipment and luggage, they plodded doggedly on. Each bend of the road brought spectacular vistas of rugged slopes and glistening snow. However, the Scouts were in no mood to enjoy or comment upon the scenery. The luminous dial of Miss Ward's wristwatch revealed that already it was well after nine o'clock. Everyone was dead tired.

Judy, Miss Ward and Ardeth took turns breaking trail. Frequently the huge drifts rose waist high. Sometimes the crust held their weight, but more often they plunged down at least to their knees. Each fall was exhausting.

Most disturbing of all, the girls noted that no one seemed to have passed along the road since the last snow had fallen. Unspoken fear began to assail them as they grew increasingly aware of their isolation.

Then Judy, who again was in the lead, abruptly halted.

"There it is!" she exclaimed. "The lodge!"

Everyone halted to stare in the direction Judy pointed. The log building was off to the right of the twisting road, perched precariously on the side of Old Candy Mountain. Against the sky it stood out as a great hulking black shape, circled by undisturbed mounds of snow. The low roof was frosted like a white cake, while great icicles hung from the eaves and half-hidden window ledges.

"Dark!" cried Beverly.

Her nerves tried to the breaking point, she dropped her skis and collapsed on top of them in the snow.

Judy put down her own belongings and tried to pull the weary patrol leader to her feet.

"Leave me alone, Tenderfoot!" Beverly snapped.

"You'll freeze in that damp snow!" Judy remonstrated. "We're all tired and discouraged, but we have to keep going."

"We have to keep going—where?" Beverly mocked. "On to Maple Leaf Lodge? The place is deserted as anyone can see. Or do we walk all the way back to Weston?"

"Beverly!" Miss Ward reproved. "After all—"

Maple Leaf Lodge

"Oh, I know, a Girl Scout is supposed to be cheerful! Always look on the bright side. But when there is no bright side—"

Kathleen slipped an arm about Beverly's waist, helping Judy pull her up out of the cold snow. "Get a grip on yourself," she advised, not unkindly. "Giving up or complaining only makes a bad situation worse."

"And maybe it's not so bad," Judy suddenly cried. "I think—yes, I do believe I see a light!"

"No!" cried Betty Bache in disbelief. "Where?"

"I don't see anything," Miss Ward declared, peering hard at the big black shape against the mountainside. "Are you sure, Judy?"

"I—I don't see it now," Judy admitted. "But when I spoke, I was certain I did. Just for a minute. I saw a moving light on the second floor."

"You imagined it," Beverly asserted. "We may as well start back to Weston right now. A pity Mr. Hawkins couldn't have waited long enough to see whether or not we would be stranded here!"

"Since we've come so far, we'll go to the lodge," Miss Ward decided. "It would be foolish indeed to turn back without making certain that the place is deserted."

"Old Caleb Shively may only have gone to bed," Kathleen commented hopefully.

"Why, of course!" exclaimed Ardeth. "How stupid of us not to think of that! The hour seems early to us, but here on the mountain folks probably go to bed at sunset."

"On to Maple Leaf Lodge!" cried Judy. "I'm sure I saw a light!"

Spurred by new hope, the girls moved quickly on through the drifts. But they discerned no light as they scanned the icecoated windows of the sprawling Boy Scout lodge.

Miss Ward pounded with her fist on the heavy front door. She succeeded only in dislodging a long icicle which had hung precariously from a ledge drectly above the stoop.

"No use, I'm afraid," the Scout leader acknowledged. "Girls, I can't tell you how sorry I am about the way this expedition has turned out. All arrangements were made far ahead."

"It's not your fault," Virginia Cunningham assured her quickly. "Anyway, we're tough and can take it!"

"All our troubles will seem funny, once we're back home," Ardeth added with as much good humor as she could muster.

"My feet are simply freezing!" Beverly said with a little whimper. "My fingers too—they're so numb I've lost all feeling."

"Here, take my mittens," Judy offered, stripping them off.

"Oh, I couldn't do that," Beverly protested, rather ashamed of herself.

Maple Leaf Lodge

"I have an extra pair," Judy said casually. "Put them on and don't worry about it."

"We have a long walk down the mountain," Miss Ward said. "I guess we may as well get started."

"First, before we go, I want to make a tour around the building," Judy said. "I was so sure I saw a light as we came up the road."

"Hurry," Miss Ward advised. "We'll wait here where it's sheltered."

Leaving her equipment behind, Judy disappeared from view. A moment or two passed and then the waiting Scouts heard a jubilant shout.

"Say, maybe she's aroused someone!" Kathleen cried hopefully. "That Judy is a gem!"

Quickly following the trail made by the Tenderfoot, the girls struggled around the corner of the building. Judy was spied at the rear of the lodge, staring up toward the sloping roof.

"I do see a light!" she cried. "It's dim and must come from a candle. But someone is in the lodge!"

"Praise be!" shouted Virginia.

"Let's pound the door down!" cried Betty, her pep returning.

Now that Judy pointed it out, everyone could see the light in the upstairs room. Their hope revived, the girls rattled the doors, both at the front and rear of the building.

"We're making enough noise to awaken the dead!" Kathleen exclaimed. "Why doesn't that sleepy old caretaker let us in?"

"Maybe he's deaf," Betty said with a nervous giggle.

"I'll arouse him," Judy said determinedly.

She rolled a snowball, packing it hard. Her first toss missed the bedroom window. But the second ball found its mark, striking the pane squarely.

The girls saw the light move. Then it went out entirely.

"What gives?" Kathleen demanded indignantly. "Does that old caretaker think we're playing hide and seek?"

Judy hurled another snowball. It cracked hard against the glass, but this time it brought results.

The window suddenly was raised, and a man peered down at the group in the yard. His face was shadowed so that the girls obtained only an impression of a cropped head of hair and a square-set jaw.

"What's the idea?" he shouted down. "What do you want?"

"Let us in," Miss Ward entreated. "We're half frozen."

"This lodge is closed. Besides, it's not open to the public."

"We're not the public," Virginia Cunningham shouted back. "We're the Girl Scouts."

"And we have a right to be here," added Betty Bache. "We've reserved the lodge for a week."

"That's right," called Beverly impatiently. "Hurry

Maple Leaf Lodge

up and let us in, please! Don't keep us standing out here in the cold."

The man had thrust head and shoulders through the open window. But he made no reply as he continued to scrutinize the group below.

Finally, he called down in an unfriendly voice: "I don't know anything about any Girl Scouts. This place is closed for the winter."

"You're Caleb Shively?" Miss Ward demanded.

Again there was a long silence. Then the man replied:

"Sure, I am, but I'm only the caretaker here. I can't let you in. Go away and let me sleep!"

"You were ordered to have the lodge in readiness for us," Miss Ward replied. "We've come a long distance, anticipating a nice outing here. We're tired and cold. You must let us in."

"I've no authority."

"Mr. Medford, the Boy Scout leader, must have written you."

"I've had no orders."

"Then if you haven't, it must be because you've not been to Weston to pick up your mail," Miss Ward said firmly. "I'm sorry to be insistent. However, the girls are too tired and cold to hike back to town. Let us in, please."

The Scouts were afraid that the caretaker would refuse their leader's request. He was silent a long while, thinking over the matter.

Finally, he said irritably: "All right, you can stay for the night. I'm warning you though, you won't find it pleasant here. And in the morning, you'll have to take your duds and leave."

The window slammed shut.

"Pleasant old soul," Betty Bache remarked. "We're about as welcome as a swarm of fleas!"

"What a wonderful time we'll have here," Beverly muttered, stamping her feet to try to restore circulation. "That is, *if* he lets us stay."

"It could be a lot worse," Ardeth said cheerfully. "Right now, if it hadn't been for Judy, we'd be wearing out our socks hiking back to Weston!"

"Oh, Judy saved the day. No question about that." Beverly's voice was edged with sarcasm. "She's a perfect gem! How the Beaver Patrol ever limped along without her I'm sure I don't know."

Chapter 6

A Night's Lodging

FOR a long while the Scouts clustered in a tight, shivering group at the lodge entrance, waiting impatiently for the old caretaker to let them in.

They could see his light moving through the dark building, but it seemed to take him an age to reach the front door.

Finally, they heard a key turn in the lock. The door swung inward on screeching hinges.

A thin man, unshaven, wrapped in a heavy woolen robe much too large for him, peered out at the girls. In the flickering light of the candle, weird shadows played over the prominent cheek bones of his face.

"Now, hold on," he commanded as Miss Ward started to pass into the lodge. "We got to discuss this."

"There is nothing to discuss," Miss Ward replied firmly. "We engaged the lodge for a week and made our reservation long in advance."

"No one told me about it," the man muttered. "The lodge is closed."

"We're cold and tired," Miss Ward returned. "I'm sorry to insist, but I have a responsibility to the girls. We must remain here for the night. Tomorrow

The Girl Scouts at Penguin Pass

we'll straighten matters out if there has been a misunderstanding."

Unwillingly, the caretaker moved aside so that the girls could enter the building.

"You won't like it here," he muttered. "The place isn't fixed up."

Stomping in out of the snow, the girls found themselves in a great bare room. Rugs had been removed and the rustic furniture loomed ghost-like, shrouded by protective sheets.

"It's cold as a tomb in here," Beverly protested. "Can't we have a fire?"

"You could if there was wood," the caretaker replied indifferently.

"There's wood enough," Judy commented, depositing her suitcase near the empty, cavernous fireplace. "I noticed it stacked by the fence as we came in."

"I'm not dressed to go out after it," the caretaker muttered. "When I'm here alone, I only keep the kitchen warm."

"On to the kitchen, girls!" Judy directed gaily. "While you're warming your toes, I'll get in a supply of wood for the fireplace."

"And I'll help you," offered Kathleen. "Once we get a big fire going, this place won't seem so dreary."

The two girls brought in several armloads of wood. Mr. Shively did not offer to help them. Nor was he very adept at kindling the fire. Noticing how

A Night's Lodging

awkwardly he worked, Miss Ward herself took over the task.

"I've been sick lately," he muttered in apology. "For two weeks I've hardly been out of bed."

"I suppose that explains why you didn't get word of our reservation here," Miss Ward remarked. "You're feeling better now?"

"Some. I'm not able to do much work though. I'm too weak to look after a crowd of giddy girls."

"We don't consider ourselves giddy," Virginia asserted indignantly.

The wood had caught well, and a warm, cheerful glow now prevailed in the immediate area of the fireplace. Judy found the electric light switch and snapped it on, but the room remained in semi-darkness.

"No lights?" she inquired.

"The line snapped in an ice storm ten days ago. Haven't been able to get a repairman up here."

"There are plenty of candles I take it?" Miss Ward questioned.

"A few."

"Will you find a supply for us?" the Scout leader requested. "We'd like to be assigned to our rooms and turn in as quickly as possible. We're all dead tired."

"You can stay over night," Mr. Shively consented grudgingly. "But in the morning you'll have to go back to Weston. As I said, I'm in no condition to

The Girl Scouts at Penguin Pass

look after a pack of girls. Besides, there are no supplies on hand."

"We'll meet tomorrow when it comes," Miss Ward repled. "Now may we have the candles, please?"

Mr. Shively disappeared into the kitchen and was gone a long while. At length he returned with seven candles which he doled out to the girls. He also brought a single oil lamp which provided much better illumination for the gloomy lounge room.

Meanwhile, the girls had divested themselves of their heavy snowsuits and had gathered about the cackling fire. Even in the uncertain light, Judy noted that Caleb Shively appeared spry and active, despite his unwillingness to be of service. He appeared to be in his late forties, much younger than she had expected.

"I guess we should introduce ourselves," she said cheerfully. "Miss Ward is our leader. Beverly Chester is patrol leader."

"I'm Kathleen Atwell."

"Call me Betty Bache."

"My name is Virginia Cunningham."

"If you forget their names, just call them the 'A-B-C's," Judy laughed. "Atwell-Bache-Cunningham. Catch on?"

"Why, Judy, you've coined a nickname for the girls," Miss Ward chuckled. "The A-B-C's. I like that!"

A Night's Lodging

"Don't forget me," Ardeth Padgett reminded the group, emerging from a shadowy corner of the room. "I demand recognition."

"Meet Ardeth Padgett," Judy concluded the introductions. "She's always good humored, and a darling."

The caretaker merely stared at the girls and grunted. However, he gazed at Judy with intent curiosity.

"And who are you?" he demanded.

"Judy Grant. Tenderfoot Scout."

"Humph," Mr. Shively grunted. "You're the one that'll give me a hard time. I know the type!"

"Judy's tops," Kathleen said loyally. "Mr. Shively, when you get to know her better—"

"I'm not aiming to know any of you better," the caretaker snapped. "As I said, you can stay tonight, but in the morning, you'll all have to leave. Now I wish you'd get settled for the night."

"We'd like nothing better," said Miss Ward quietly. "Where do we sleep?"

"You got your own bedding, I see."

"Yes, we came prepared. Lucky for us we did."

"Follow me."

Taking the oil lamp. Mr. Shively guided the girls up an old stairway and along a balcony which overlooked the main lodge room.

He opened a door at the head of the stairs. Stale, cold air blasted the girls in their faces.

"Two of you can sleep here," he said. "A room for four adjoins. And there's another room next to it."

"I'll take this one," announced Ardeth, who was eager to settle herself. "That is, if no one else wants it. Who wants to bunk with me?"

"I do," declared Virginia, starting back down the stairs for her luggage.

Betty, Miss Ward and Beverly took the larger room, leaving the other double one for Kathleen and Judy.

"Now don't be racing around, once you get to bed," Mr. Shively scolded. "I want it quiet because I need my sleep."

"We'll try not to disturb you," Miss Ward said dryly. "About breakfast—"

"There won't be any," the caretaker growled. "I told you I'm out of supplies. You'll have to go to Weston."

Mr. Shively shuffled off, taking the oil lamp with him. He tossed more wood on the fire in the lodge room below, before disappearing in the direction of his own quarters over the kitchen.

Kathleen and Judy carried their suitcases into the room assigned to them. Without a fire in the grate, it was a cheerless chamber, cold, dusty and damp.

"No use unpacking," Kathleen said dispiritedly.

A Night's Lodging

"We'll be leaving early in the morning."

"Maybe not," Judy returned, testing the mattress of the upper bunk. "You know, I'm beginning to like Maple Leaf Lodge despite all our bad luck. The skiing must be wonderful here."

"No food," Kathleen reminded her. "No reservation. Nothing. If Mr. Shively were more obliging—"

"Queer about him," Judy remarked, half to herself. "You know, from Ted's letters I pictured Mr. Shively as a nice, friendly old man."

"He's exactly the opposite."

"Strange the Boy Scouts would tolerate such an old grouch, Kathy. Maybe it's just Girl Scouts that he can't bear."

"He seemed to take an especial dislike to you, Judy."

"So he did." Judy grinned ruefully as she unwrapped her bed roll. "Oh, well, I'm too tired to let it bother me. I'll take the upper, Kathy. Feel as if I could sleep a million years."

"Judy—"

"At your service."

"I just wanted to say—" Kathleen groped for words. "—Judy, you were splendid today. You may be a Tenderfoot, but you certainly proved that you can take it. Now, a certain person I could mention—"

"Don't!" Judy stopped her. "I was just trying to

put the third Scout law into practice: *A Girl Scout's duty is to be useful and to help others.* Well, here I go!"

She climbed nimbly into the upper bunk and pulled the blankets snugly around her. For a moment she lay very still, listening to the whistle of wind around a corner of the rambling building.

"Judy—"

"Uh-huh," came the sleepy response.

"Now that we're alone, I wish you'd tell me what it was your brother Ted wrote about this place."

"Nothing about the lodge, Kathy."

"Penguin Pass then."

"It really wasn't so much," Judy replied reluctantly. "Maybe I exaggerated the situation."

"You're hiding something. And you're not the type that gets nervous over nothing either! Come on, give!"

"Ted mentioned a mystery here on Candy Mountain," Judy answered.

"You told me that much before."

"Well, it concerns a plane crash that occurred while Ted and the other Scouts were here at the lodge," Judy began.

She did not go on, for even as she spoke, the silence which had fallen upon the lodge, suddenly was shattered. From a nearby bedroom there came a shrill, ear-splitting scream.

Chapter 7

Mystery and Mice

JUDY sat upright in the bunk, listening intently. "What was that?" she demanded. "A scream from the next room!"

"It sounded like Virginia's voice!" Kathy declared, clutching the blankets.

Judy swung herself out of the upper bunk, snatching up a woolen robe. She groped for her shoes, and finding them, clattered across the bare floor with Kathy close behind.

The hallway was dark, and the only discernible light came from the flickering flames of the dying fire in the lodge room below the balcony.

From the bedroom shared by Virginia and Ardeth there came an excited babble of voices. Judy rapped sharply on their door and then flung it open.

"What's wrong?" she demanded. "Who screamed?"

"Well, for crying out loud!" Kathy exclaimed. In the shadowy light she had spied Virginia perched on a dusty table, her bare feet drawn up monkey-fashion beneath her.

Ardeth, on the other hand, was laughing hysterically.

"Don't come in here with bare feet," the plump girl warned. "You'll regret it if you do."

"Who screamed?" Judy asked again.

"I did," Virginia admitted weakly. "I-I couldn't help it."

"But what happened?"

By this time, Miss Ward and the other members of Beaver Patrol had reached the bedroom, all demanding to know the cause of the commotion.

"I-I was starting to make up my bunk," Virginia explained, her teeth chattering. "I unrolled the mattress and out ran—a mouse!"

"A mouse!" chuckled Betty Bache. "An innocent little mouse! And you frighten us half out of our wits!"

"At the very least, we thought you'd seen a ghost," added Kathleen.

"I guess you wouldn't have thought it was so funny, if it had happened to you! He jumped practically into my hand! Furthermore, I'm sure there's a nest of them in the mattress!"

"Silly!" scolded Betty. She was an amateur naturalist and had no dislike for mice, snakes, bugs or animals. "Come on down off that table."

"Not until I'm sure the mice are gone."

"Someone hold a flashlight for me, and I'll check," Betty offered.

"I will," Judy volunteered. "I haven't any love for mice myself though."

"Virginia slipped up on one of the Girl Scout laws," Ardeth teased her. "Be Kind to Animals."

"A mouse isn't really an animal," Virginia defended herself. "Anyway, I wasn't unkind to him. I just retreated to this perch."

The other girls kept a safe distance away as Miss Ward, Judy and Betty made a thorough inspection of both mattresses.

"There was a nest here," Betty said after exploring the mattress on Virginia's lower bunk. "But the mice are gone now. I guess your screams frightened them away, Virgy."

"I'm sorry," Virginia apologized, coming down off her table perch. "I didn't mean to awaken the household, or rather, disturb it before anyone had a chance to settle down. That scream just slipped out."

"You'll be all right now?" Miss Ward asked. "If you would prefer to sleep in another room, I'll change bunks with you."

"I'll stay," Virginia said resolutely. "That is, if you're sure all the mice are gone."

"Positive," Betty reassured her.

Ardeth and Kathleen were making up the bunk for Virginia when heavy footsteps were heard along the inner balcony.

"What goes on here?" demanded the gruff voice of the caretaker.

Miss Ward met him at the bedroom door. She

The Girl Scouts at Penguin Pass

explained what had occurred and apologized for the disturbance.

"I wish this place would quiet down," Mr. Shively muttered. "When I heard that wild scream I thought—"

"I'm sure it won't happen again," Miss Ward said. "Do excuse us this time."

The caretaker merely grunted. He waited until the girls had returned to their rooms before padding off to his own quarters.

"Ho-hum," Judy mumbled drowsily as she climbed up into her bunk once more. "What a night!"

"And no breakfast tomorrow," Kathleen reminded her. "We'll have to get up early and hike to Weston."

"Maybe not."

Without amplifying the remark, she burrowed down beneath the blankets, and almost immediately was lulled into deep slumber by the cozy warmth of the covers.

It was much later when Judy awakened. She felt completely refreshed and for a moment thought that it must be nearly morning.

But she saw that the bedroom windows were dark, and that dawn still was far away. What had awakened her?

The moon had struggled out through a heavy matting of clouds, casting a cold, etherial light over the sparkling snow. Wind whistled eerily around the

Mystery and Mice

corners of the lodge. The branches of a barren tree, moving back and forth, scratched the building and made weird shadows on the room walls.

Peering over the edge of the bunk, Judy noted that Kathy was sleeping as peacefully as a child. The room was very still. Yet she could not free herself of the feeling that an unusual sound had disturbed her.

She lay for awhile, staring at the dark beamed ceiling, listening. Suddenly, her muscles became taut. Every sense alert, she strained to hear. Distinctly, she could hear the soft creak of floor boards.

Was someone moving stealthily along the inside balcony? One of the girls perhaps? Or Miss Ward?

The sound was a heavy one, almost as if a weight were being dragged along the creaky floor boards.

Judy lay quiet, reluctant to leave the warmth of her bunk to investigate.

"It's nothing," she told herself. "I'm getting the jitters, that's all. If Ted hadn't written that letter about Penguin Pass—"

On the floor below, a door distinctly opened and closed.

Startled, Judy now fully aroused herself. She found her warm robe, and throwing it over her shoulders, slid down from her high perch.

Moving swiftly to the window, she looked out upon the great expanse of sparkling snow. She could see no one.

59

"Maybe it wasn't a door that closed," she told herself. "Or it might have been Mr. Shively going outside for more wood."

The bed chamber was freezing cold. Shivering, Judy went to the balcony overlooking the lodge room, and peered down.

Nothing seemed amiss. All the doors along the hallway were closed. A fresh log had been consigned to the fireplace.

"I must have heard Mr. Shively stirring around," Judy decided in relief.

Her curiosity satisfied, she returned to her own room. As she entered, Kathy stirred restlessly.

"Anything wrong, Judy?"

"No, go back to sleep."

Nimbly, Judy climbed up into her own bunk. Once more she snuggled down, but sleep did not come quickly. The old lodge seemed fairly alive with strange noises.

"I'm giving myself a bad case of the jitters," she informed herself sternly. "Relax, Tenderfoot! Get yourself a little shut-eye. You'll need it tomorrow."

Despite the admonition, she could not sleep. Finally, a little after six o'clock, she abandoned the attempt.

"At least I may as well make good use of my time," she decided. "I'll surprise the girls!"

Dressing quietly so as not to awaken Kathy, she tiptoed from the room.

Chapter 8

Penguin Pass

NOT until seven-thirty the next morning did Maple Leaf Lodge begin to stir with life. Hearing a flutter of footsteps along the inner balcony, Kathleen aroused herself lazily.

"Hey, Judy, time to get up!" she called.

There was no answer.

Kathleen spoke again. Still receiving no reply, she pulled herself out of bed into the cold room. Only then did she discover the upper bunk empty.

Flinging open the bedroom door, she peered out into the balcony. It was warmer there, and in the room below, a great fire blazed.

Ardeth and Virginia, fully dressed, were descending the stairs.

"Gracious, I must have overslept!" Kathleen exclaimed. "Where's Judy? Has anyone seen her?"

"She's been as busy as a bee!" Ardeth reported gaily. "That girl! She's not a Tenderfoot! She's a diamond in disguise."

"What's she done now? Started the fire, I see."

"Oh, she wheedled Mr. Shively into that," Virginia chuckled. "Judy's rustling breakfast for the gang!"

"Breakfast! But I thought there were no supplies!"

"Judy's found some!" Virginia chuckled. "Trust her

for that. Just hurry and get dressed, so you don't keep us waiting."

"I'll be down in a flash," Kathleen promised.

Ten minutes later when she clattered down the stairway to the kitchen, the room was abuzz with excited conversation.

Judy herself, a large chef's apron over her new Scout uniform, was frying slices of ham at the wood stove.

The table was neatly set. At each place there was a dish of canned fruit and dry cereal.

"Sorry, no eggs this morning or cocoa," Judy informed the group. "You'll have to use canned milk for the breakfast food. But it's better than walking to Weston for breakfast."

"Judy, you're marvelous!" Betty Bache praised lavishly. "Where did you find that wonderful ham?"

"In the cupboard. There's a good supply of canned foods."

"Mr. Shively told us he had no supplies."

"I figure he said that because he doesn't want us to stay," Judy replied, lowering her voice. "For some reason, he's allergic to Girl Scouts."

"We have a perfect right to be here," Virginia flared. "What did he say when you found the supplies, Judy?"

"Nothing."

"Where is he now?" Miss Ward inquired. "I want to talk to him about our stay here."

"He was around a few minutes ago. Maybe he's out getting more wood. I invited him to eat breakfast with us, but he refused. The truth is, he's very annoyed at me, for getting into the supplies."

"Let him fuss!" Betty snorted. "Does he expect us to starve?"

"I'll see to it that anything we use is replaced," Miss Ward declared. "After all, as the caretaker here, he should have some interest in making us comfortable."

By this time the ham had been fried to delicate perfection. There was no milk available except the canned product, but Judy had brewed a large pot of tea.

Breakfast was a gay meal. Every scrap of ham disappeared and the girls made short work of clearing up the table.

"Now you've done more than your share, Judy," Betty shooed her out of the kitchen. "Virginia and I are doing the dishes."

"What's the plan for the day?" Ardeth anxiously asked Miss Ward. "Do we go or stay?"

"I've given considerable thought to it," the Scout leader replied. "We paid for use of the lodge and our reservation was approved. I had hoped for a comfortable stay here. We ran into a bit of trouble and even if we obtain permission to remain, living here for a week may be somewhat rugged."

"Fun, nevertheless," Judy interposed.

"It's up to you girls," Miss Ward went on. "If you want to stay, I'll go to Weston this morning and try to put a telephone call through to Mr. Medford, the Scoutmaster. What do you say?"

"Let's remain if we can!" Virginia urged. "I'm beginning to like it here—especially when someone cooks my breakfast."

"We could load in plenty of supplies," added Betty.

"How do you feel about it, Beverly?" Miss Ward asked, turning to the patrol leader.

"I don't think my opinion matters with the girls."

"Nonsense, Beverly! Of course it does."

"Personally, I'd just as soon return home," Beverly said. "It's so cold and disagreeable here, and Mr. Shively doesn't want us—"

"The weather will moderate," Kathleen broke in. "Besides, if we all pitch in and work, we can clean the lodge and get it decently heated. I say, let's stay."

"You see?" Beverly shrugged. "I knew the girls would disagree with me. But if they want to stick, it's all right."

The matter was taken to a vote. With exception of Beverly, all the girls registered a desire to remain at Maple Leaf Lodge.

"Well, that's settled then," Miss Ward said. "I'll hike down to the village right away. Beverly, would you like to go with me?"

"All right," the patrol leader agreed, without enthusiasm.

"We may be gone for several hours," Miss Ward continued. "While we're away, Judy is in charge here."

"Judy—" Beverly started to protest. However, she thought better of it and lapsed into silence.

While Betty and Virginia were doing the dishes, Miss Ward talked to Mr. Shively. The caretaker did not take kindly to the plan of having the patrol remain at Maple Leaf Lodge in the absence of its leaders.

"Why don't you all go to Weston?" he urged. "I've no authority to let anyone remain here. I don't like it."

"By noon at least, I should be in touch with Mr. Medford," Miss Ward replied. "Then you'll have your orders, one way or the other."

Mr. Shively continued to argue the matter, but the Girl Scout leader quietly but firmly over-ruled him. The hike down the mountain to Weston would not be an easy one, and she was not inclined to ask any of the girls to make it unnecessarily.

After Miss Ward and Beverly had gone, the girls set to work dusting and cleaning the lodge. Mr. Shively regarded their activity with increasing disapproval.

"How's the skiing hereabouts?" Judy asked him.

"Fair."

"Any good trails to Penguin Pass?"

The caretaker eyed the girl coldly. "Penguin Pass is closed," he told her. "Besides if you have good sense you won't go near that place."

"Why?"

"Because it's dangerous. The snow lies heavy on the slopes. A careless skier could start a bad snow slide and be buried."

"Cheerful thought!" Judy responded. "I hadn't any intention of skiing at Penguin Pass. I was merely curious, that's all."

She began to put on her heavy galoshes, ski trousers and mittens.

"Where you going now?" Mr. Shively demanded suspiciously. "Penguin Pass, I'll warrant! Tell a youngster they're not to do something, and certain as fate that's what they want to get at!"

"Oh, Penguin Pass doesn't interest me at the moment," Judy rejoined pleasantly. "I'm only going outside to look around a bit. I need fresh air."

"I'll go with you," Mr. Shively volunteered.

Though Judy would have preferred to be by herself, the caretaker followed her out into the crisp, cold morning air.

The girl stood for a moment, gazing at the vast expanse of cream-colored snow that sparkled in the sunlight. Long, blue shadows extended in slim fingers down the mountainsides.

"Over yonder is the ski chair tow," Mr. Shively

pointed out, indicating a slope some distance to the right of the main highway. "Best way to reach it is by car to Bledlow's Inn. If you're aiming to stay at Candy Mountain, you might get reservations there."

"We have reservations—here," Judy responded with emphasis.

"You aren't staying," the caretaker retorted.

Judy paid no heed, but began to wade through the deep drifts along the side of the lodge.

"Where you think you're going now?" Mr. Shively demanded.

"To check the telephone wires."

"What's the use of doing that?" the caretaker asked, thoroughly annoyed. "I told you, didn't I, that a load of ice snapped off the wire."

"When was that?"

"A night or two ago."

Judy saw for herself that a long line which ran from a pole on the main road, was down in the snow. The wire had broken off close to the lodge.

"Have you reported this to the telephone company?" she inquired.

"I told you I haven't been to town."

Judy inspected the broken wire briefly and then turned her attention elsewhere.

"What's that big building to the right?" she questioned. "A barn?"

"You guessed it."

"Any stock?"

"One old horse."

"Really?" Judy's eyes sparkled. "What's his name?"

"It's a she. Mollie."

"Oh, may I see her? I like horses. Besides, if I take care of an animal for a week, I win a merit badge. I'd like to become a Second Class Scout and to do it, I have to earn a great many badges."

"Well, you aren't going to start on Old Mollie," Mr. Shively announced flatly. "Stay away from the barn. You understand?"

Judy stared at the caretaker in surprise. "You don't like me much, do you?" she inquired.

"You're nosy," he replied disagreeably. "I don't want anyone poking around here."

"Sorry," Judy said. "The Girl Scouts aren't aiming to make life unpleasant for you. We planned an outing here, and we feel we should be entitled to stay."

"Well, you've got to leave," the caretaker insisted doggedly. "The sooner the better."

Judy made no reply. She trampled around the entire lodge. At the rear exit she paused, noticing long marks in the snow.

Apparently, a heavily-laden toboggan had been dragged through the drifts from the lodge to the nearby barn.

Mr. Shively noticed Judy studying the tracks.

"I was hauling wood," he informed her.

"From the barn?"

"I got some stached there. Keeps it dry."

"But the toboggan was loaded when you were hauling it from the lodge to the barn. Not the other way around," Judy pointed out. "See! The tracks enroute to the barn are very deep in the snow, showing that the sled was heavily loaded. Coming back, it barely broke the surface of the banks."

"I suppose you know whether the toboggan was coming or going!" Mr. Shively said sarcastically.

"Certainly. Your boot tracks show that very plainly. Furthermore, the footprints aren't too fresh. They must have been made last night—"

"You give me a pain!" Mr. Shively cut in. "You and your Scout lore!"

"It's not Scout lore particularly. I just noticed—"

"You notice too much," Mr. Shively said wrathfully. "I knew the minute I laid eyes on you that you'd make trouble."

"Trouble?"

"Oh don't pretend to be so innocent," the caretaker snapped. He stamped off through the snow.

"Oh, about that toboggan," Judy called after him. "Is it in the barn? The girls could have some fun if you'll let them use it."

Mr. Shively pretended not to hear. He disappeared into the barn, however, closing the heavy door behind him.

Judy started to pursue the caretaker, then abandoned the idea. No use antagonizing him further. Obviously, he disliked her and resented her questions.

After wandering about the yard for awhile, she went into the lodge again. All the work now had been done, and the girls were seated around the fire.

"We've just elected you chief cook, Judy," Kathleen informed her. "Think you can rustle up something for lunch?"

"Easily," Judy replied. "The supplies are ample."

"I wonder why Mr. Shively told us he didn't have any?"

"Oh, he wants us to leave, that's obvious."

Ardeth, who had a clear view of the window, now observed the caretaker leaving the barn on snowshoes.

Watching, the girls saw him haul the toboggan Judy had requested, to the side door. Then he struck off across the fields on his snowshoes.

"Wonder where he's going?" Betty speculated.

"Not to Weston, that's certain," Virginia answered. "He's going the opposite direction."

"Toward Penguin Pass," Judy supplied. "Or at least in that direction."

"We'll be here alone," Ardeth remarked, somewhat nervously. "Our wood won't last too long. He might at least have told us where he's going and how long he expects to be away."

"We won't need him," Judy said. "Let's prepare lunch. After that, we can haul in our own wood."

The girls set about inspecting the stock of canned

goods and planning the noon meal. Under Judy's direction, they prepared a simple but excellent repast of corned beef hash, scalloped tomatoes and stewed prunes.

After the dishes had been wiped and stacked away, time began to drag.

"Shouldn't Miss Ward and Beverly be here by now?" Betty worried.

"It may take some time to reach Mr. Medford," Judy pointed out. "I don't look for them back for a couple of hours yet at least."

"How about getting in more wood?" Virginia proposed restlessly.

"And then we might do a little exploring," added Betty. "Why waste such a beautiful day?"

From the woodpile by the fence, the girls carried in a large assortment of logs, kindling and slab wood. The toboggan which Mr. Shively had left for them provided a handy means of transportation.

"Now let's have some fun!" Ardeth proposed when the work was finished. "We could hike to the main road to meet Miss Ward and Beverly."

"Why not trail Mr. Shively?" Kathleen proposed, pointing out the track his snowshoes had left in the snow. "It would be interesting to learn where he went."

"And have him more furious than ever at us!" Judy chuckled.

"Oh, we won't need to trail him very far. Besides, he's been gone hours."

The Girl Scouts at Penguin Pass

"Okay, it might be fun at that!" Judy agreed. "Let's go!"

Without showshoes of their own, the girls discovered that it was not easy to walk across the huge drifts. Sometimes the snow held their weight, but often enough, they plunged through.

A fairly strong wind from the north swept across the fields. Fine snow drifted into the tracks Mr. Shively had made. Finally, it no longer was possible to follow his trail.

"We may as well turn back," Judy advised the group. "We've come quite a distance from Maple Leaf Lodge now."

"What lies just ahead?" Kathleen inquired curiously.

The girls stood in a particularly picturesque valley, hemmed in with evergreens, and sheltered from the wind. Kathleen's attention had been drawn to a narrow trail, leading off to the left, and marked by a rustic sign.

"Let's see what it says," she urged her friends.

On they trudged to the entrance of the trail. With a mittened hand, Kathleen brushed snow from the signpost so that the words could be distinguished.

A silence fell upon the group. The trail was marked Penguin Pass, and a tiny black arrow pointed up the steep, snowy slope.

Chapter 9

A Snowman Guard

"SO this trail leads to Penguin Pass," Kathleen remarked, staring curiously up the untrodden path.

"Let's push on and see what it's like," urged Betty Bache.

"Hold on!" Judy stopped her. "The trail might be miles long."

"If it is, we can turn back."

"It's late now," Judy argued. Besides, I don't think we should explore this particular trail without talking it over first with Miss Ward."

"Why not?" Betty demanded. "Are you afraid we might get lost?"

"Perhaps."

"That's silly. We know how to mark a trail if there's any need for doing it. But how could we lose our way unless there are branch-offs?"

"I just don't think we should attempt it," Judy said.

"But why?"

Judy was reluctant to reveal the real reason behind her unwillingness to explore the trail. She remained silent.

"I guess you're afraid of the steepness of the trail. Is that it, Judy?"

"Well, the climb looks rather difficult."

"We're all seasoned hikers," Virginia said. "I vote that we go on."

"So do I," laughed Betty. "How about you, Kathy?"

"Judy is in charge while Miss Ward is away. I'm in favor of letting her decide. Besides, I think she's right."

"You believe it wouldn't be a safe trail?" Ardeth asked in amazement.

"Something like that."

Virginia, Betty and Ardeth were astonished by the firm attitude taken by Judy and Kathleen. Though at first, Penguin Pass had interested them only mildly, their curiosity now had been whetted.

"You two girls are acting mighty queer," Betty accused. "You know something about Penguin Pass that you're keeping from us!"

"Not I," Kathleen denied.

"Judy then. What do you know, Judy?"

"Only that my toes are getting cold." Judy replied, dancing up and down in the snow. "Shall we start back to the lodge?"

"You're really firm about not going on?"

"Yes, I feel it would be unwise."

"But it's not late yet," Betty launched a final argument. "We'll have a tedious wait at the lodge if we return now. I wish we'd worn our skis. Then we could have practiced."

A Snowman Guard

"Let's make a snowman," Virginia suddenly proposed. "If we can't explore the trail to Penguin Pass, why not set up a guard at the entranceway?"

"Fine!" approved Betty. "I'll make the head."

The girls began to roll huge balls, pyramiding them one upon another at the trail opening. Betty fashioned a fierce looking face, using bits of broken sticks for eyes, nose and mouth.

"Monstro," she announced the snowman's name. "That's what we'll call him. He really does look as if he were guarding the trail, doesn't he?"

"Sort of," Judy admitted absently. "Now that the snowman is finished, shall we get started back to the lodge?"

"My, but you're eager to get us away from here," Virginia remarked. "What's your hurry, Judy?"

"None, except that it's growing late."

"And this place makes you uneasy. You weren't in any special haste until we hit the trail to Penguin Pass."

"Let's hit it for the lodge instead, shall we?" Judy suggested. "Miss Ward and Beverly should be there by now. They'll wonder what became of us."

She started off the way they had come, and the others reluctantly followed. Once beyond the protecting rim of evergreens, the hikers again were assailed by a biting wind. It nipped their cheeks and forced them to lower their heads for protection.

"I guess Judy was right about turning back," Betty

acknowledged, fighting for breath. "I never dreamed it would be so hard walking into the wind."

Maple Leaf Lodge, snuggled on the slope, was a welcome sight. The girls stomped in, shaking snow from their clothing.

Mr. Shively was there before them, ensconsed in a comfortable chair before the fire. His shoes were off and he made no move to put them on as the Scouts came in.

"We had a wonderful hike!" Betty declared brightly. "All the way to the trail that leads to Penguin Pass!"

"Penguin Pass!" Mr. Shively looked directly at Judy. "I thought I warned you about that place!"

"Oh, Judy didn't want us to explore the trail," Virginia said quickly. "Mr. Shively, is there any reason why we shouldn't?"

"The trail is dangerous. It's steep and rocky. Besides, there's danger of starting snow slides."

"So early in the winter?" Judy inquired mildly. "I thought the slides usually came with the spring thaws."

"You know everything," Mr. Shively retorted. "I'm telling you to stay away from Penguin Pass, that's all."

"Did you ever hear about a plane crashing anywhere near there?" Kathleen inquired.

Judy was flashing warning signals which went unnoticed.

A Snowman Guard

Mr. Shively eyed Kathleen intently. "What was that?" he demanded.

"Judy mentioned it," Kathleen returned. "I never did get the straight of the story."

"It was nothing," Judy said. "My brother told me that a passenger plane crashed somewhere near the pass. Three passengers were killed, I believe. One man disappeared. Or at least his body never was recovered."

"No wonder you didn't want us to take that trail, Judy!" Betty exclaimed. "Is the wreckage still there, Mr. Shively?"

"Of course not," the caretaker replied. He was scowling at Judy, plainly annoyed at her for having revealed the information.

"What became of the missing passenger?" Ardeth questioned.

"How should I know?" Mr. Shively muttered. "I was away when the accident occurred."

"Did the plane catch fire?" Virginia inquired.

"Not that I heard of," Mr. Shively answered reluctantly. He squirmed uneasily and reached for his shoes.

"Then how could a passenger just disappear?"

"You got me," the caretaker muttered. "It never was any of my concern."

"Was there never any investigation?" This question came from Ardeth.

"Of course, there was! Government men came in

and checked the wreckage. All the passengers were accounted for, so far as I know. That talk about a man disappearing was mostly wild rumor."

"It would be sort of interesting to visit Penguin Pass," Betty remarked thoughtfully. "I'd like to see where the big plane crashed."

"There's nothing to see," Mr. Shively informed her. "The wreckage all has been removed. The trail is a long one—tough to climb."

"Even so, I'd like to try it," Betty insisted.

Mr. Shively could not hide his exasperation. "Well, you won't get the chance!" he retorted. "You girls are leaving here today. In fact, if your leader doesn't come soon, I'm putting you out bag and baggage."

"You couldn't do that," Judy said quietly.

"You'll see! I've given you enough warning. If you want to stay on Candy Mountain tonight, you'll have to make reservations at Bledlow's Inn."

The girls gave up attempting to talk to the caretaker. After warming themselves for awhile, they read some of the old magazines the Boy Scouts had left behind the previous summer.

Finally, Kathleen and Judy donned their ski suits, announcing that they intended to walk to the main road.

"Miss Ward and Beverly should have been here long ago!" Judy said anxiously. "I hope nothing has happened to them."

A Snowman Guard

"If they aren't here in thirty minutes, you're all going to Weston," Mr. Shively announced in a grim tone. "I'll not put up with another night like the last one!"

Once Kathleen and Judy were outside, the pair remarked upon the caretaker's unpleasant personality.

"Even if we should get to stay, he'll make it hard for us," Kathleen remarked. "We seem to have rubbed him the wrong way."

"I aroused his ire this morning by suggesting that I'd like to take care of Mollie," Judy said, smiling at the recollection."

"Who is she?"

"A horse. Stabled in the barn."

"Poor thing! I'll venture Mr. Shively doesn't attend to her very well."

"Let's look at her, shall we, Kathy?"

The girls took the footpath which led to the big barn. There they found their way barred by a pair of stout doors which refused to swing inward. A padlock had been attached to a metal hasp, making it impossible to enter the barn without a key.

"I suppose the barn doors are kept locked so the horse can't be stolen," Kathleen remarked, rattling the padlock.

"Maybe," Judy agreed. "Only I wonder why Mr. Shively waited until we came to install the hasp?"

"What makes you think he did?"

Judy pointed to the wood on the barn door. At one place close to the hasp, there were freshly made, unweathered marks. Clearly, someone had attempted to put the metal piece at one point, and then shifted it to another location.

"Why, it does look as if the hasp and padlock had just been put on!" Kathleen exclaimed.

"Mr. Shively did it since we came," Judy said. "I'm sure of it! He intends to make certain that we don't bother Mollie or anything in this barn. And if you ask me, it's an insult to the integrity of the Beaver Patrol!"

Chapter 10

The Reluctant Caretaker

JUDY and Kathleen were thoroughly annoyed to discover that the barn had been padlocked.

Although they had not been particularly eager to inspect the stable previously, they now were far more determined to do so.

"Why do you suppose Caleb would lock us out?" Judy speculated. "Is he afraid we'll take something or maybe let Mollie out of the barn?"

"It must be he's afraid the horse will get away," Kathleen replied. "But that's unjust. He should know that Girl Scouts are dependable. I guess we'd know enough not to leave the door open or unlocked."

"It's plain enough that he installed the lock after we came," Judy went on. "I maintain it's an insult to us. I think I'll speak to him about it!"

"Better let it ride," Kathleen advised. "Already he's in a ferment because we're here. If we let him quiet down, he may become cooperative."

"Maybe, but I doubt it." Judy frowned thoughtfully. "That caretaker isn't the cooperative type. Funny thing! Ted said the Boy Scouts set great store by him."

"Well, doesn't that indicate that he must have good qualities buried down under?"

"They're buried all right, Kathy," Judy laughed.

Leaving the vicinity of the barn, the two girls trudged toward the main road. The trail made by the patrol the previous night still was faintly visible, and they followed it to the junction of the private road with the main highway.

By this time early twilight was beginning to creep down the mountainside. Vague shadowy shapes cast their silhouettes upon the expanse of snow.

"Night is coming on early," Judy observed uneasily. "I wish Miss Ward and Beverly would come soon!"

"So do I," Kathleen agreed, climbing a rail fence. "If they don't, I have a hunch Mr. Shively will keep his word and send us all back to Weston for the night."

As far as the girls could see down the road there was no sign of Miss Ward or Beverly. The afternoon rapidly was turning colder. After sitting for awhile on the fence, the two Scouts began to feel the chill penetrating their woolen clothing.

"Shall we go back to the lodge?" Kathleen shivered. "No use waiting here."

"Let's take a jog down to that first bend in the road," Judy suggested. "I want to be sure they're nowhere in sight."

To restore circulation in their numbed toes, they dog-trotted most of the way. By the time they

The Reluctant Caretaker

reached the bend, they were warm again, and laughing.

"Look!" Judy cried pointing down the mountain road. "A sled!"

"It looks like Mr. Hawkins too!" exclaimed Kathleen jubilantly. "Someone is with him."

A few minutes later after the team had made another turn in the road, the girls were elated to discern that the passengers were Miss Ward and Beverly.

Soon the sled came up and the old storeman called out a cheery greeting as he helped the girls aboard.

"We were beginning to worry," Judy told Miss Ward. "You were gone longer than we expected."

The Scout leader explained that she and Beverly had delayed their start back from Weston nearly an hour so that Mr. Hawkins could help them with the supplies they had ordered.

"Then we're staying!" Kathleen cried. "Oh, I'm so glad!"

"I hope we're staying," Miss Ward said, a bit grimly. "I've had rather a day of it at Weston. However, I think matters have been cleared up."

The Scout leader related that upon reaching Weston that morning, she and Beverly first had checked at the postoffice. There they had found considerable mail for Maple Leaf Lodge and in particular a letter of instruction to Mr. Shively from Barton Medford, the Boy Scout master in Fairfield.

Upon discovery of the unopened letter, Miss Ward next had placed a long distance telephone call to Weston. But as luck would have it, Mr. Medford had been out of town.

"We were told he wouldn't be back at Scout Headquarters until later afternoon," Miss Ward went on. "I couldn't telephone the lodge to let the girls know. All Beverly and I could do was wait."

"It was tiring too," Beverly contributed. "Such a sleepy, one-horse town! Nothing to do but walk up and down main street!"

"I didn't mind, except that I worried about the girls," Miss Ward said. "Judy, is everything all right at the lodge?"

"Oh, yes! Mr. Shively has been threatening to put us out, of course."

"He can't do that. I'm armed with authority now."

"Then you finally got through to Mr. Medford?"

"Yes, at four o'clock. He was very upset that his message to Mr. Shively hadn't been picked up at the postoffice. The upshot of it was, he said we're to stay, and if conditions aren't satisfactory, he'll make a reduction in the charge for the lodge."

"That's decent of him," Judy declared. "What about Mr. Shively?"

"I have the letter of instructions for him. Further-

The Reluctant Caretaker

more, Mr. Medford said if he makes the slightest trouble, I'm to telephone him. He'll come here personally."

"While we were at Weston, we reported the telephone being out of order," Beverly added. "The company promised to have a repair man here tomorrow or the day following."

"We bought ample supplies too," Miss Ward resumed, indicating the cardboard boxes piled in the sled. "Milk, fresh vegetables, meat and fruit. Mr. Hawkins kindly offered to help us with our load."

The sled now pulled up at the entrance to the private road.

"End of the line," Mr. Hawkins called out cheerfully. "If someone would dig out a few of those biggest drifts, I could get my horses through and drive right to the door."

"We'll take care of that tomorrow," Judy promised. "Now that we know we're to stay, we'll shovel paths and make the place look like home."

Mr. Hawkins unloaded the boxes for the girls.

"Sure you can manage?" he asked.

"Oh, it's not far to the lodge," Kathleen assured him. "We'll make it all right."

Laden with the boxes, the four trudged slowly toward the distant building, which in the gathering dusk looked peaceful and wintery against the mountainside.

It was hard going with a heavy load. Everyone was heartened when Kathleen spied the other Scouts coming to meet them with the toboggan.

"They must have seen us from the window!" she exclaimed in relief. "Praises be!"

With many hands to help, the boxes quickly were transported to the lodge kitchen. Mr. Shively watched disapprovingly as the girls began to store their purchases.

"A letter for you, Mr. Shively," Miss Ward said, offering him the one she had brought from the Weston postoffice. "This will explain everything, I think."

In silence, the caretaker read the communication. Still without comment, he stuffed the sheet of instructions into his pocket.

"Well?" inquired Miss Ward pleasantly. "Now that you have official word from Mr. Medford. I hope you feel better about us being here."

"The lodge isn't fixed up," the caretaker muttered. "You'd be more comfortable at the inn. If it's the cost you're worried about, I maybe could fix it with the manager to get you a rate."

Miss Ward stared at Mr. Shively in astonishment. "You really don't want us here," she said, half-accusingly.

"Ma'am," the caretaker responded, "I've nothing against you or your patrol. I—I like being alone, that's all. All summer I have to ride herd on a bunch

The Reluctant Caretaker

of Boy Scouts. A man sort of looks forward to a quiet winter by his own fireside. Then to have a pack of girls descend on him like a blizzard out of the sky—well, it's upsetting."

"I appreciate your point of view," Miss Ward replied. "You feel that in a way we've invaded your privacy."

"That's it," Mr. Shively said quickly. "Now you'd be comfortable at the inn. I'll pay whatever it costs."

From his billfold, the caretaker peeled off a hundred dollars in a single denomination. Amazed at the amount of money the man had on his person, the girls could only stare.

"Here, take this," he said, offering the bill to Miss Ward. "Just leave me to myself. It's all I ask."

Miss Ward did not accept the money.

"You place me in a most difficult position," she said. "I dislike to intrude upon your privacy. On the other hand, you were employed here as a caretaker, and it is your duty to open the lodge to all comers who have a right to be here. Mr. Medford instructed me to remain. He said if you made the slightest trouble to let him know and he'd come up here at once to straighten out the difficulty."

Mr. Shively replaced the money in his billfold.

"That won't be necessary," he said gruffly. "If you're dead set on staying, then stay! I was only thinking about your comfort. You won't like it here."

"But we do!" Judy cried.

"Just see that we're well supplied with wood and we won't bother you for anything else," declared Virginia. "We'll take care of the work."

With the supplies Miss Ward and Beverly had brought, the girls prepared an excellent supper. They invited Mr. Shively to join them in the meal, but he turned down the invitation.

Later, however, after the dishes had been done, they heard him poking about in the kitchen ice box, and correctly guessed that he was helping himself to some of their tastily prepared left-overs.

Grouped about the crackling fire in the main lodge room, the girls sang songs and told stories. Judy interested herself in an old stack of books and magazines. In the pile she came upon a photograph album left behind by the Boy Scouts.

Immediately, as she let her discovery be known, the other girls clustered about to see and chuckle over the pictures.

"There's one of the Scoutmaster, Mr. Medford." declared Miss Ward. "How different he looks in his swimming trunks!"

"Ted must be in here somewhere," declared Judy, flipping page after page. "Yes, here he is, with a couple of older boys. And some man too! I wonder—"

She speculated no further, for at that instant, there came a loud crash from the direction of the kitchen.

"Gracious!" Kathleen exclaimed. "What was that?"

As the girls listened, they heard a low moan as if someone were in pain.

"Mr. Shively must have hurt himself!" Judy cried, dropping the photograph album. "Come on! Let's see what happened!"

Chapter 11

A Photograph Album

ALARMED by the loud crashing noise, the Girl Scouts all rushed to the kitchen.

Mr. Shively stood in the wavering candle light, nursing his cut left hand. A glass water pitcher lay shattered on the floor.

"Oh, you've hurt yourself!" Ardeth exclaimed.

"It's cut bad," the caretaker moaned. "I was reaching for the pitcher and knocked it over. A piece of glass is lodged in the flesh."

Miss Ward called for Ardeth to fetch the oil lamp from the living room. Under its brighter glow, she quickly examined the cut.

"I can't find any glass," she asserted. "The wound isn't very deep."

Nevertheless, she sent Virginia to get iodine and bandages from her first aid kit. While she was wrapping Mr. Shively's hand, Judy and Kathleen carefully swept up the broken bits of glass and wiped the wet linoleum.

"Much obliged," the caretaker mumbled after his hand had been wrapped. "I'm going to bed now to get some rest. It's been a hard day."

"You made a long trip on snowshoes," Judy reminded him.

A Photograph Album

The caretaker shot her a quick, annoyed glance but made no reply. Taking the oil lamp for his own use, he shuffled off toward the bedroom above the kitchen.

"Beverly and I neglected to buy additional oil lamps while we were in Weston," Miss Ward said regretfully. "We had so many things to think about. Tomorrow, if the telephone is repaired, I'll call and have Mr. Hawkins send them. Or better still, we may be able to have the electric wires repaired."

Deprived of all but candle light, the girls decided to follow Mr. Shively's example and retire early. Judy helped Betty and Miss Ward bank the fire for the night.

"Mr. Shively isn't much use to us," the Scout leader remarked, as she placed the fire screen before the hearth. "In fact, he seems rather lazy. Now that he has a cut hand, I'm afraid he'll do even less to make the lodge comfortable."

"The cut isn't deep, is it?" Judy inquired.

"A mere scratch. I wouldn't have wrapped it, save that there's always a danger of infection if the skin is broken."

"Why do you suppose he made such a fuss?" Betty speculated. "He seemed to crave attention."

"It's amazing to me that Mr. Medford would keep him here as a caretaker," Miss Ward said, careful to lower her voice so that it would not carry. "His years of association with Boy Scouts doesn't seem to have contributed much to his fund of useful information."

"Perhaps he's pretending," Judy theorized. "He didn't want us here, and he may be trying tricks to make us leave."

"In that case, we'll surprise him," Miss Ward declared. "We'll show him what good sports Girl Scouts can be. Well, to bed now! We want to be up early, so we can get in a full day of skiing."

The cold outdoor air had made all the girls rather drowsy. Judy bounced into her bunk with a deep sigh of relief.

"Mr. Shively didn't say where he went today on snowshoes," she remarked drowsily. "He's a queer one!"

"That's a highly complimentary term for him," Kathleen rejoined. She stood at the window, gazing out across the snowy roof which sparkled in the faint moonlight. "Well, what do you know!"

"What now?" Judy demanded, sitting up in bed.

"Mr. Shively said he was going to sleep, didn't he?"

"He did."

"Well, look at him now!"

Already Judy was down out of the bunk, and across the room. Peering through the light film of frost on the window, she saw a man midway to the barn, framed against a background of glittering snow.

A Photograph Album

The man had donned a heavy jacket, mittens, and wore the huge ear muffs which the girls secretly regarded as ridiculous.

"What's he doing out there at this time of night?" Judy demanded.

"It's not so late," Kathleen replied. "Only he said he was going straight to bed. I guess that cut isn't bothering him much."

As the girls huddled at the window, they saw the caretaker go directly to the barn. He fumbled with the padlock on the door, unlocked it and went inside.

"He must be looking after Mollie," Kathleen said. "I guess that's the one responsibility he takes seriously."

"I'd like to see that old horse," Judy declared. "I have a hunch Mr. Shively hasn't been giving her good care. He may be afraid we'll find out about it and report to Mr. Medford."

"There's something queer about the way he acts," Kathleen agreed. "Why does he take such pains to keep us out of the barn?"

"I'm going to get in there," Judy announced determinedly. "Just wait!"

"We could sneak down there now—"

"Too late," Judy said with a sleepy yawn. "By the time we dressed, he'd be out again and have the doors locked."

"You're right," Kathleen agreed a moment later.

"He's coming now."

The caretaker came out of the barn, closing the doors behind him. After fastening the padlock, he tramped back to the lodge, quietly letting himself in the back way.

Judy and Kathleen heard him moving softly about on the lower floor. Creaking boards told of his retreat to the bedroom over the kitchen. Then the dwelling became quiet.

"Goodnight," Judy mumbled, scrambling up into her bunk again. "I'm off to dreamland. Even if a ghost parades up and down the balcony all night, it won't bother me."

She fell asleep almost the moment her weary body touched the mattress, hearing no further sounds throughout the night.

Bright sunlight streamed through the frosty windows, when finally Judy opened her eyes. Someone was pounding hard on the door.

"Seven o'clock?" she murmured, trying to struggle up.

"Eight!" called Betty Bache who was at the door. "Make it snappy or you'll be late for breakfast."

"Be with you in a jiff," Judy promised.

She leaped out, pulling the covers off Kathleen. The chill of the room made them dress with lightning speed. Anticipating a day outdoors, both put on several layers of light woolen clothing beneath their ski suits.

A Photograph Album

Miss Ward, Virginia and Ardeth had taken their turn preparing breakfast. The kitchen was cozily warm from the wood stove. Eggs were frying in a large iron skillet and there were corn muffins in the oven.

"Where's Beverly?" Miss Ward asked, testing the muffins. "Breakfast is practically ready."

"She's coming down the stairway now," Virginia reported. "It takes her an age to dress."

"It does not," Beverly retorted, hearing the remark. "I couldn't find one of my socks, that was what delayed me."

"If you'd put things away—" Virginia began, then realizing that she was being critical, checked herself. Breaking off, she inquired: "Shall we invite Mr. Shively to join us at breakfast?"

"It might save broken glassware," Ardeth said with a chuckle. "I'll call him."

She went to the doorway, intending to call up the stairway. To her surprise, the caretaker already was downstairs. He stood suspiciously close to the kitchen door, and it struck Ardeth that he might have been listening to the conversation.

"Mr. Shively, would you care to join us for breakfast?" she invited him.

"Don't mind if I do," he returned cheerfully. "Those eggs smell good."

"How is your hand this morning?"

"Only fair," Mr. Shively responded, making a

grimace as if in sudden pain. "The wound is sore and stiff. I won't be able to do any work with it for a day or two."

Ardeth had her own opinion of Mr. Shively's ability to work, but she held her tongue. The girls politely made room for him at the table, and offered him the platter of eggs before taking any themselves.

Mr. Shively scooped three onto his plate and helped himself to two corn muffins. He ate with relish, unaware or unconcerned by the fact that in taking more than his share, he had shorted the girls.

"You aiming to ski this morning?" he asked, stuffing half a muffin into his mouth.

"That is our plan," Miss Ward replied. "Have you any suggestions?"

"Try the trail over by the inn," he advised. "The ski tow runs from ten until four o'clock."

"How about Penguin Pass?" Judy inquired mischievously.

The caretaker regarded her with intense annoyance. "I told you to stay away from there!" he said irritably. " Can't you get it through your head that the trail is dangerous?"

"I was only kidding," Judy said, getting up from the table. "Relax, Mr. Shively! We'll probably try the ski lift."

"But it's a long hike to the inn from here," Kathleen remarked. "Perhaps for a day or two, we could practice near the lodge, before venturing on the

A Photograph Album

inn trails. I imagine they're rather difficult except for professionals like Judy!"

"You won't find any good skiing hereabouts," Mr. Shively discouraged her. "If I were doing it, I'd pack a lunch and make a day of it at the inn. Or you could get your meal there in the dining room."

"You wouldn't be trying to get rid of us for the day?" Judy teased.

"No such thing." Mr. Shively denied. "Do as you please! I know you will anyway!" He stomped out of the kitchen.

"There, I rubbed his fur the wrong way again," Judy sighed. "I always say the thing that excites him!"

"He certainly doesn't like you," Kathleen replied. "Whenever he's in the room, I see him watching you —almost as if—"

"As if what, Kathy?"

"I was going to say, almost as if he were afraid of you."

"But why should he be afraid of me, Kathy? That doesn't make sense."

"There's something about you that seems to make him uneasy. Or maybe it's just his nature."

Beverly and Betty had started to do the dishes, so Ardeth, Kathleen and Judy assigned themselves to cleaning up the living room.

"Say, we never did see the rest of those Boy Scout photographs," Kathleen remarked as she

The Girl Scouts at Penguin Pass

dusted the fireplace mantel. "What did you do with the album, Judy?"

"I left it where I was sitting."

"In which chair?"

"By the fire." Judy crossed the room to look for the album. "That's funny. It's not here."

"You were sitting there," Ardeth recalled. "I remember very well."

"When Mr. Shively let out a yell, I just dropped the album," Judy said thoughtfully. "After that, we all went to bed."

"Well, it's here somewhere," Kathy said.

A search of the living room did not disclose the missing album. Judy carefully sorted through all the magazines and papers to make certain the photograph book had not been closed between other pages.

"Maybe you took it to your room," Kathy suggested.

Judy shook her head. "No, I'm sure I didn't. But I'll look to make certain."

She returned a moment later to report that the missing album was not in the bedroom. Ardeth and Kathleen meanwhile, had consulted Miss Ward and the other girls. All denied having seen the album or having examined it since the previous night.

As the loss was being discussed, Mr. Shively came in. Judy asked him if he had seen the elusive photograph book.

A Photograph Album

"No, I haven't," he replied shortly. "If it's gone, don't blame me."

"Oh, I wasn't," Judy assured him.

"The Boy Scouts set great store by that album," the caretaker muttered. "They won't like it, if it's gone."

"It must be here in the lodge," Judy said, rather desperately. "I know I didn't lose it myself."

"Judy, think hard," Miss Ward advised. "Are you sure you left the album in the chair?"

"I did. I know I did. Someone—"

Judy flushed and lapsed into silence, thoroughly ashamed of the thought which had come to mind. She had started to say that someone deliberately had taken the album to plague her. Beverly perhaps.

"The album will turn up," Miss Ward said pleasantly. "Don't worry about it, Judy."

"I can't help but worry," Judy replied. "I'll find it though! I'll do it, even if I have to move every stick of furniture in the lodge!"

Chapter 12

A Locked Stable

MOST of the morning was spent on the gentle slopes near Maple Leaf Lodge. Miss Ward and Judy helped the other girls with their skiing technique, demonstrating snowplow turns to left and right, jump turns and stem christies.

Worn from so much exertion, the somewhat plump Ardeth finally collapsed on her back in the snow.

"I'm going to make 'Angels'," she announced. "That's more in my line."

She moved her arms up and down in the snow, leaving an impression of angel wings. Their imaginations inflamed, the girls temporarily abandoned their skis and did likewise.

"I can improve on that!" laughed Judy. "Watch!"

By skillful rotation of both arms and legs in the snow, she patterned the familiar trefoil emblem of the Girl Scout organization. Then with her finger, she traced in the letters "G.S." at the top.

"Trust Judy to go us one better," Beverly Chester drawled. "She always does."

The laughter and sparkle of fun faded from Judy's smoothly tanned face. She said quietly:

"I'm sorry, Beverly. I wasn't trying to show off."

A Locked Stable

"What's better than making the Scout emblem?" Ardeth demanded, quick to go to Judy's defense. "I'm going to try it."

Soon all the girls were making a series of the figures in the snow. Even Miss Ward attempted one. But Beverly would not. She remained coolly aloof, pretending to check the bindings of her skis.

At lunch time, the girls returned to the lodge for a hot meal and to rest their tired muscles. While the others assisted Miss Ward with the meal or stretched their legs by the fire, Judy resumed her search for the missing photograph album.

"I simply can't understand what became of it," she remarked. "You don't suppose it could have been tossed into the fire by mistake? Perhaps with some old newspapers?"

"That could have happened," Virginia agreed. "Don't worry about it, Judy. If it doesn't show up by the time we leave here, we'll have to write Mr. Medford that's all."

"Anyway, it wasn't your fault," added Kathleen. "We all were looking at it."

Lunch finished, the girls stacked away the dishes and then discussed the afternoon program. Beverly favored hiking to the inn to try the ski lift. However, Miss Ward vetoed the suggestion, pointing out that it would be much better to make the trip the following day when an early start could be made.

"Then what can we do this afternoon?" Beverly

asked restlessly. "More skiing around here, I suppose."

"If the girls like," Miss Ward agreed. "I must admit I'm rather bushed myself. I think I'll lie down for a couple of hours."

"Me too," chimed in Ardeth.

The others still had a reserve of energy and decided to accompany Beverly. Judy, the first to get into her ski suit and heavy boots, wandered outside ahead of her friends.

A path had been shoveled to the barn, and she was surprised to note that the door was slightly ajar.

"Mr. Shively must be there now," she thought. "This is my chance to see Mollie!"

As she opened the barn door wider, Mr. Shively heard her cough. In the act of giving the horse a few ears of corn, he uttered a startled exclamation.

"You!" he entoned.

"Little me," Judy agreed brightly. "How's Mollie this afternoon?"

"I thought I told you to stay away from this barn," Mr. Shively said. "You can't take a hint, can you?"

"I only wanted to see Mollie." Judy went over to the mare and patted her neck. Mollie nuzzled her hand.

"She needs currying or something, doesn't she?" Judy asked, troubled to see how shaggy the mare's coat appeared. "And she seems cold. Don't you have a blanket?"

A Locked Stable

"Will you get out of here and mind your own business? I'll look after the horse."

"But she's cold standing here without any exercise," Judy argued. "There must be a blanket somewhere in the stable. Up in the mow perhaps." She started toward the ladder which led to the loft.

Mr. Shively blocked her way. His lean face now was convulsed with anger.

"You git out!" he ordered, and his voice was ugly. "Of all the Girl Scouts, you're the worst! You're a snoop and a pest! Now get out and don't come back here again. Understand?"

"Y-Yes, sir," Judy backed away. She was more hurt than afraid, though she had never witnessed such an unwarranted display of temper.

"You may mean all right, but you're a nuisance," Mr. Shively said in a somewhat milder voice. "You always have to pry."

"I didn't mean to, Mr. Shively. I was only worried about Mollie. It's cold here in the barn, and she needs exercise."

"I'll see that she gets it, and a blanket as well," the caretaker promised. "Just keep out of my hair, that's all I ask. Now beat it!"

He followed Judy out of the barn, padlocking the door again.

Close to tears, she walked away from him to join the girls who had just come out of Maple Leaf Lodge.

"Where have you been, Judy?" Kathleen inquired curiously.

"Prying, I guess. That's what Mr. Shively called it."

"You were at the barn."

"Yes, but not long. He drove me out."

"Did you see the horse?"

Judy nodded as she put on her hickory skis. "I thought Mollie needed a blanket, but Mr. Shively told me to mind my own affairs. I-I guess that's my trouble. I try to manage things. Probably that's why Beverly—"

"No such thing," Kathleen contradicted quickly. "You're not one bit bossy, Judy. Now forget Mr. Shively. He has a chronic case of ingrown personality!"

In a few minutes all the Scouts had gathered and were ready to start for the slopes. Beverly took the lead and the other girls followed, gliding along with smooth, shuffling motions.

For awhile, the group skied on a slope not far from the lodge. Beverly, who did not have very good form, repeatedly tore down the hill, skiis apart, her poles swinging wildly.

"Track! Track!" she yelled, and the other girls scrambled out of her way.

"Someone should tell her!" Kathleen muttered after Beverly had nearly knocked Virginia to the

A Locked Stable

ground in her uncontrolled flight. "Judy, why don't you—"

"No, thanks," Judy declined with a laugh, "I've already put my foot in it several times. After all, she's the patrol leader."

"And should know better, but doesn't."

Judy helped Kathleen and Betty with stem christies, and then tiring of the sport, the girls became interested in animal tracks.

Betty identified those of a squirrel and a cat and a rabbit. The latter tracks they followed for a short distance.

"Say, where is that trail leading to Penguin Pass?" Beverly inquired curiously. "Not far from here, is it?"

"Pretty close," Virginia replied. "We built a snowman there yesterday."

"You did! Let's see if he's still there!"

"It's rather a long hike," Virginia started to protest and then shrugged indifferently.

Single-file, led by Beverly who seemed in unusually high spirits, the girls proceeded to the point of demarcation for Penguin Pass.

From a distance they could see the big snowman standing guard at the entranceway to the break amid the pine trees.

"He's still there!" Betty shouted in high glee. "I wish we'd brought a hat and a man's coat for him."

"Monstro is too large for the garments of any mere human," Virginia chuckled. Eagerly she started on, hoping to be the first to reach the trail entrance.

Judy, however, with her effortless, long glide was there ahead of the entire group. When the others came up, they found her staring at something in the snow.

"Footprints!" she directed the attention of her companions. "Footprints of the snowman!"

Amazingly, a long trail of very large human shoe prints led from the base of the snow figure up the trail toward Penguin Pass.

"Well, did you ever!" exclaimed Betty, bending down to examine one of the footprints. "These have been made since we were here yesterday."

"And they're huge!" Judy declared. "One would think they'd been left by a giant!"

"By Monstro, the snowman," supplied Virginia. She stooped to measure one of the prints with her hand. "Why, it's at least a foot and a half long! No human being has a boot that size."

"Judy, you sneaked out here early this morning and played a joke on us!" Kathleen accused her chum. "'Fess up."

"On my honor as a Scout, I swear I didn't," Judy returned soberly. "I haven't been near here since yesterday."

"Well, someone must have done it as a joke."

"This is no time for silliness," Beverly said. "If

A Locked Stable

anyone in the Beaver Patrol is responsible, speak up."

Only silence followed her request for information. Then Judy spoke.

"It's queer about these footprints," she said. "We saw none along the trail as we came up. And there are none beyond."

"Only on the path leading to Penguin Pass," Kathleen noted. "The man, or giant, or whatever it was, must have come down from the pass to find the exit blocked by our snowman guard. Then he turned and went back."

"But the footprints are only going *away* from the snowman," Betty pointed out.

Judy had been surveying the immediate surroundings. The snow had been trampled considerably so that there was a confusion of boot and ski tracks. Nevertheless, she was able to discern other tracks which definitely had not been made by any member of the Beaver Patrol.

Following Judy's gaze, Kathleen too, noted the footprints of a man with normal size shoe.

"Those tracks don't explain a thing," she said, divining her chum's thought. "The snowman's prints are simply huge."

"What do you make of it, Judy?" Betty asked in perplexity.

"I can't figure it out. The prints are so large."

"There's a simple way to solve the mystery," Beverly announced. "We can follow the prints and discover where they go."

"Toward Penguin Pass," Kathleen said, staring doubtfully up the snowy trail.

The locality was a lonely one. Tall evergreens, caked heavily with unbroken snow, stood like stern sentinels on either side of the winding trail.

"Well, what are we waiting for?" Beverly demanded, digging in her poles. "Let's go!"

Virginia and Betty hesitated and then started to follow. Kathleen and Judy held back.

"Well, aren't you coming?" Beverly flung impatiently over her shoulder. "Or are you afraid?"

The taunt brought color to Judy's wind-tanned cheeks.

"I'm not afraid," she replied. "But you know we've been advised to stay away from Penguin Pass. Before we venture over a trail which may prove dangerous, I think we should learn more about it."

Chapter 13

A Forbidden Trail

BEVERLY regarded Judy with a wooden, stubborn expression.

"I don't see any reason why we shouldn't try this trail," she argued. "We wouldn't need to go very far. If there appeared to be the slightest danger, we could turn back."

Judy said nothing, staring at the huge footprints which extended from the base of the snowman as far as one could see up the forbidden trail.

"One can't tell what we'd run into," she said slowly. "That man, or creature, or whatever he is, may still be up the path somewhere in the vicinity of Penguin Pass."

"Besides, Mr. Shively advised against the area," Kathleen supported her chum.

Beverly's angular jaw stiffened in a stubborn line. "So we have to do exactly what Mr. Shively says! He's been so helpful to the Beaver Patrol since we came here."

"Mr. Shively has nothing to do with this," Judy said.

"No, it's a matter of common sense," argued Kathleen. "The trail could prove dangerous."

"I don't see how," Beverly argued. "It may be

a bit steep but we can be careful, can't we? As for those footprints, they must have been made by a man with a very large shoe."

"I never saw such a large print in all my life," Betty Bache declared uneasily. "Perhaps Beverly, it would be better to wait—"

"Until we're back home, I suppose," Beverly cut in. "Not for me, thank you. We only have a few days here, and I wasted the first one going to the village with Miss Ward. This trail intrigues me and I intend to learn more about it. If the rest of you are afraid, wait here for me."

"We can't do that, and you know it," Virginia said. "If you're determined to try it, then I'll go with you."

"So will I," Betty agreed reluctantly. "We won't have to go very far, I guess."

Beverly now waited for Judy and Kathleen to make their decision.

"I suppose I'll go along too," Kathleen said reluctantly. "How about you, Judy?"

"I have no choice."

"You can rush back and report to Miss Ward," Beverly said unpleasantly.

"You know I wouldn't." Judy tried to cover the hurt but the other's words had stung deeply.

"Okay, let's go!" Beverly declared, jubilant that her will had prevailed. "Follow me!"

She shuffled off around the guardian snowman

A Forbidden Trail

and up a narrow winding opening between the sentinel pines. The others followed single-file, Judy bringing up the rear.

The trail rapidly became more difficult, rounding snowy cliffs which gave breath-taking views of a peaceful valley below. Now and then the girls caught a glimpse of the tall church spire from Weston, but the mountain blocked their view of Bledlow Inn and the ski chair lift.

Beverly climbed doggedly, following the huge footprints which had intrigued her. "It's hard to tell which set were made last—those going up, or the ones coming down the path," she remarked, pausing a moment to catch her breath.

"Those going up look the fresher to me," Judy said quietly. "We're five to one, but even so—"

"Afraid we'll meet Monstro, the giant man?" Beverly goaded her.

"No, but I admit I have an uneasy feeling about this place. If we'd seen anyone in the area today it wouldn't seem so baffling."

"After we left the lodge, I saw Mr. Shively out on snowshoes," Virginia recalled. "But if he came this way, he circled around to avoid passing us on the practice slope."

"These are shoe tracks, not those made by regular snowshoes," Kathleen pointed out. "Besides, Mr. Shively wears a comparatively small boot. I noticed."

"All the same, he's the only one we've ever seen come this way," Virginia responded.

Small, sharp rocks hidden in the snow, impeded the progress of the girls as they moved on. Judy was the first to remove her skiis. Upending them in a deep snow bank, she announced her intention of picking them up on the downward trip.

"No use ruining good hickory runners," she remarked.

"The going is getting more difficult all the time," Kathleen commented, directing the remark at Beverly.

The patrol leader, however, gave no sign that she had heard.

Following Judy's example, the other Scouts removed their skis and left them behind.

Even without them, walking became increasingly difficult. At times the trail was bare of snow, then again, the girls sank through the drifts above their knees. In the higher altitude, they were more aware of the chill air which penetrated their woolens.

As they tired of the climb, the girls lost zest for the adventure. Twice Virginia suggested that they abandon the investigation and turn back. Each time Beverly vetoed the suggestion.

"I want to find out more about these mysterious tracks," she declared stubbornly.

"If we should meet the giant who made them, we might regret it," Betty said, pulling her scarf more

A Forbidden Trail

tightly about her neck. "Why, I don't believe a human could have such a huge foot! It's uncanny."

"All the more reason we should find out about it," Beverly argued.

"Scouts are supposed to use good judgment," Kathleen reminded her. "It seems to me we're venturing in here completely unprepared—"

"No such thing. Why, if we should encounter anyone or anything, we're five to one! If you're afraid, turn back."

Kathleen's eyes blazed, but she held her temper in check. Without replying, she trudged doggedly on.

Presently, Judy paused to gaze thoughtfully up at the mountainside, banked heavily with unbroken snow. She now had moved up to third position in the line, and her halt temporarily gave those behind a chance to catch breath.

The trail had twisted and turned in such a confusing manner, that Judy was not entirely certain of her direction. In her mind's eye, she visualized that Penguin Pass must lie a considerable distance ahead and that it could be entered only through a narrow gap between the mountain peaks.

"What's wrong now?" Beverly demanded, looking back over her shoulder. "Winded, Judy?"

"Not exactly."

"Then why hold up the march?"

"I was just looking at the slope above us, Beverly.

There's a lot of snow up there."

"Naturally."

"Furthermore, it wouldn't take much to dislodge it. A skier might turn the trick by accident."

"Well, no one is skiing above us," Beverly retorted carelessly. "It's not thawing today either. So why borrow trouble?"

"I was only trying to stave it off by looking ahead—"

Beverly gazed directly at Judy with no trace of a smile. "Tenderfoot," she drawled, "I wish you wouldn't work so hard at living up to the Scout manual. Sometimes it's rather a strain on the rest of us. After all, I'm the patrol leader and the responsibility is mine."

"That snow does look sort of ominous," Kathleen declared, siding with Judy. "A little jar might set it off. I heard Mr. Shively warning Miss Ward to watch out for slides."

Beverly reached down, and gathering up a handful of snow, packed it tightly into a ball. She hurled it far up the mountainside, in a contemptuous gesture which expressed her opinion of the protests.

"Don't do that, Beverly!" Kathleen said sharply. "The snow is melting today, or you couldn't have packed that snowball so easily. If that snow field should start moving—"

"Oh, Judy has given you a case of the jitters!" Beverly retorted. "There's as much danger of a rain

A Forbidden Trail

storm as there is an avalanche. Come on, let's hit the trail!"

Beverly struggled on, and the others reluctantly followed single file. Now and then, as they rounded sharp turns, they obtained breath-taking views of the peaceful valley below.

But the trail of footprints seemed endless.

"Beverly, surely you don't plan on hiking all the way to Penguin Pass?" Virginia presently demanded. "It may be miles, and we didn't even bring an extra sandwich or a compass."

"It's getting late too," Betty argued, squinting at the sun as she removed her dark goggles to wipe away a mist that had formed. "Let's turn back."

"Okay," Beverly surprisingly agreed.

In truth, having proven her authority over the others, she too had lost zest for the difficult climb.

"I want to see what's around the next bend," she asserted. "Then we'll start for Maple Leaf Lodge."

"Thank goodness for small favors," Betty muttered. "My toes are half frozen now."

The girls rounded the curve and halted. Judy rather anxiously scanned the steep slopes near the timber line. She had made an alarming observation.

The footprints which they had followed so faithfully, no longer kept to the narrow trail. Instead, they led directly up the steep embankment to a line of tall evergreens.

Suddenly, Judy uttered a choked cry.

Her discerning gaze had detected a wide crack twenty or thirty feet across the slope. As she watched in horror, the crack widened.

The entire slope seemed to be moving slowly downward!

For a second, Judy stood horror-struck and paralyzed. Then she found voice.

"A slide!" she shouted. "Run! Run for your lives!"

Chapter 14

Retreat

A large section of the hillside above the girls seemed to be in motion.

With screams of fright, they retreated around the bend in the trail. Scrambling and pushing against one another in their haste, they dashed madly down the path.

A thunderous roar assailed their ears, and a cloud of snow powder and dust enveloped them. But the main part of the slide moved far to their right, missing them by a substantial margin. The snow pile crashed on down the mountainside, finally coming to rest harmlessly in the valley below.

Weak from the closeness of their escape, the girls collapsed at the side of the trail.

"It—it was only a small slide," Beverly muttered as a feeble defense for her own insistence that the party proceed. "I don't think we'd have been buried if it had struck us."

"We're safe and that's what counts," Betty gasped. "If Judy hadn't seen the snow when it first started to move—well, I shudder to think what might have happened."

"Mr. Shively was right!" Kathleen exclaimed.

"This trail to Penguin Pass is dangerous. We never should have attempted it."

"You're blaming me, I suppose," Beverly said, her lips drawing down into a sullen line. "Okay, it was my fault. But how was anyone to know that the snow would start sliding?"

"Normally, I don't think it would have," Judy declared. Her voice was strained and tense. "If you girls will wait here, I want to go back to the bend and take a look."

"It's risky," Kathleen warned.

"The snow has moved past, and I doubt there'll be another slide. I want to look at something, that's all."

"What?" demanded Beverly.

Judy did not reply, if indeed, she heard the question. While her companions waited, she retraced her way to the sharp curve in the trail. The place where the Scouts had stood a moment ago had been swept clean of snow. For a long while she scanned the slope whence the slide had started.

"Hurry, Judy!" Kathleen called to her.

Judy rejoined the group.

"Well?" Beverly demanded. "What did you discover?"

"Nothing," Judy replied. "You were right that the slide was only a small one. I wonder though, what could have started it?"

"I don't know or care," Beverly answered. "We've

Retreat

all had enough of this investigation. Let's trek for the lodge."

Going downhill was much easier, especially as the trail now had been fairly well broken. As for Beverly, the starch seemed to have gone out of her entirely. She trudged along in dejected silence although the other girls chattered nervously of their adventure and spoke wistfully of a warm fire and hot soup.

Presently, toward the exit of the path, they regained skis and poles. A short distance on and they stood once more beside the guardian snowman.

"I'm going to knock him down!" Beverly announced, raising her pole to take a whack at Monstro's head.

"No! No!" Virginia protested, grasping her arm. "Don't do it! I like the old fellow! Besides, we want Miss Ward to see our work."

"As far as I'm concerned, I never want to come this way again," Beverly muttered. "I've had my fill of Penguin Pass. Tomorrow I want to try the regular ski trails and the chair lift."

Nevertheless, she spared the snowman. Slipping into her skis, she glided off toward the lodge.

Judy, the best skier of the group, easily could have passed her. But she did not. Deliberately, she slowed her pace to that of the other members of Beaver Patrol. As a consequence, Beverly soon was far ahead.

"I don't like to talk about anyone, especially a sister Scout," Betty said as they rested a moment before taking a final run down to the lodge. "But something will have to be done about Beverly."

"*A Girl Scout is a friend to all and a sister to every other Girl Scout,*" Virginia reminded her, quoting the Scout law.

"As Beverly said, the manual can be over-done," Betty replied with a grimace. "Anyway, the point I'm making is that she constantly violates the principles upon which the organization is based. Is she courteous? Is she cheerful?"

"It's partly our own fault," Kathleen said soberly. "She didn't ask to be chosen patrol leader. That was our doing. Maybe we did make a mistake. I think our attitude has made that fact increasingly clear to Beverly, and naturally, she resents it. That tends to make her more than ever determined to show her authority as patrol leader."

"We should ask her to give up the position," Betty argued. "What do you think, Judy?"

"I? Well, I don't like to give an opinion because I don't know Beverly very well as yet. Our experience on the trail to Penguin Pass was unfortunate, but we shouldn't blame her too much. That snowslide was beyond her control."

"An act of nature, so to speak," Kathleen said with a chuckle.

"I'd not call it that either," was Judy's rather strange reply.

Virginia and Betty scarcely noticed, for already they were shoving off for the final run down to Maple Leaf Lodge. Kathleen, however, noted her companion's odd tone and expression.

"Judy," she asked abruptly, "now that we're alone, tell me what you think started that snowslide."

"I don't know."

"You have a theory though."

"Just before the slide started, I noticed a trail of those huge footprints going up the mountainside."

"Then you think our giant was up there amid the evergreens?"

"When I went back to look, I thought I saw a dark form in among the trees."

"A huge man?"

"No-o," Judy responded thoughtfully. "My impression wasn't very clear. I just saw a formless shape. Then it was gone."

"You believe someone was up there?"

"I think so, Kathleen."

"Then that's why you said the snowslide wasn't an act of nature. You think that man, or creature, or whatever he is, started the avalanche."

"Either by accident or design. I wouldn't know which."

"But why would anyone do such a thing on purpose?"

"To frighten us away perhaps, Kathleen. The slide wasn't a very big one, and I doubt it would have swept us over the trail. It didn't have enough power."

"I don't want to meet a bigger one," Kathleen declared.

Virginia and Betty had reached the fence by the lodge and were waving for the other two girls to come along. Kathleen and Judy started side by side swooping down in a controlled movement which was both swift and joyous.

In the lodge, a crackling fire drew the girls like a magnet. Miss Ward and Ardeth had supper nearly ready but its serving was delayed to permit the Scouts to relate their exciting adventure on the Penguin Pass trail.

"You shouldn't have ventured on the trail," Miss Ward chided. "I'm surprised that you attempted it without being accompanied by an experienced skier. And those footprints—"

"It was my fault," Beverly acknowledged. "I take full responsibility."

Nothing more was said that night about the near-mishap, though it was taken for granted that the escapade would not be repeated.

Miss Ward and Ardeth reported that they had spent a very quiet afternoon at the lodge, sleeping most of the afternoon. Neither the telephone company repairman nor an electric light man had appeared.

"We'll be without lights and a telephone for another day at least," Miss Ward reported with a troubled frown. "Frankly, I don't like it. If anything should go wrong here, it would take a long while to get word to the village. And if there should be a bad storm it might be impossible."

Mention of the village reminded the girls that since arriving at Maple Leaf Lodge they had not written to their parents or friends.

"We'll all go to Weston early tomorrow, and then on to Bledlow Inn," Miss Ward declared. "Write your letters and cards tonight, so you'll have them ready."

By the inadequate light of candles and oil lamps, the Scouts scribbled their messages home. Judy wrote her mother, and then on impulse, wrote another letter to her brother, Ted.

"Did you tell him about our day on Penguin Pass trail?" Kathleen teased.

"I did more than that," Judy replied. "I asked him for specific information. If he comes through with it, and a reply arrives before we leave here, I may clear up some of the mystery."

"I'd like to know about those huge footprints," Kathleen remarked. "It makes me uneasy to think that a huge giant may be lurking in the forest near here."

"A pre-historic giant perhaps?"

"Cave men weren't so large," Kathleen grinned. "This fellow must be a monster."

"Don't give it too much thought or you may have nightmares," Judy advised. She covered a yawn. "I'm bushed! Think I'll turn in. See you at breakfast."

"You'd better," Kathleen chuckled. "It's your turn to cook it again."

The night was uneventful. After a day in the open, the girls, one and all, slept as deeply as if they had been drugged.

In fact, Judy found it difficult to get the patrol members up in time for breakfast. She had poached eggs, made toast, and with Miss Ward's help, added a rasher of bacon. The food seemed to vanish the instant it reached the table.

"I see we'll need to order more supplies while we're in Weston," Miss Ward remarked. "I had hoped Mr. Shively would take the responsibility, but apparently he's not the type."

"Where's he been keeping himself?" Ardeth asked, helping herself to the last strip of bacon on the platter. "He wasn't around here yesterday. Has anyone seen him this morning?"

"He was up early taking care of Mollie," Judy contributed. "At least I saw him go to the barn. He spends a lot of time there. The horse should be grateful."

Mr. Shively came in from out-of-doors while the girls were straightening the kitchen. Learning that they were planning on going to Weston that morning, he seemed quite pleased.

"You'll have a good day at Bledlow Inn," he declared. "If you should decide to stay—"

"We'll be back here at night the same as before," Virginia cut in. "You can't get rid of us, Mr. Shively."

By nine-thirty the entire Beaver Patrol had arrived in Weston. The girls mailed their letters at the postoffice and inquired the road to Bledlow Inn. A Weston hardware dealer who chanced to be driving that way, kindly offered them a ride.

As the girls were waiting for his truck to pull up to the curb, Judy directed the attention of her chums to a man who only that moment had come out of the postoffice.

"Remember him?" she inquired.

"He's the same man who rode the bus with us," Ardeth recalled. "I wonder who he is and what he's doing in Weston? He certainly doesn't act as if he were a native here."

Just then the hardware dealer drove up with his truck, so the girls piled in, forgetting the stranger who interested them only mildly.

Soon they found themselves unloaded at Bledlow Inn, a rustic lodging place built to resemble a Swiss chalet. The building stood at one side of the main paved highway. Directly across, was the ski chair lift which carried passengers to the top of Adonis Ridge, whence descended three trails.

Before starting the ascent, the girls went into the Inn for hot chocolate. In fact, Ardeth became so engrossed in purchasing souvenirs and scenic postcards that the others scarcely could drag her outside.

As a group, the girls went down to the little wooden shack where tickets could be bought for the chair lift.

Judy and Virginia were the first to take off. They seated themselves side by side in the swinging chair, allowing their skis to rest on the bar directly beneath.

The attendant closed a protecting bar in front of them, and the chair moved up the mountainside on its steel cable.

Smoothly, they sailed through the air, obtaining a panoramic view of the entire countryside. Judy drew deeply of the invigorating, rarified air.

"Wonderful!" she exclaimed. "I feel as if I could fly!"

The chair halted with a slight jerk.

"Now what?" Virginia gasped, alarmed.

"We've stopped so other passengers can get on. A ski lift is like a ferris wheel that way."

From their swinging perch, the girls obtained a bird's-eye view of the ski trails and of Bledlow Inn. Cars parked in an adjoining lot appeared as mere specks.

Retreat

"My, we're moving up fast!" Virginia gasped as the machinery was started once more. "You know something? I'll be terrified to go down one of those trails. They're too steep."

"The beginner's slope is on the other side of the machinery house at the top of the mountain," Judy explained. "I know because I asked the attendant. We'll be able to see it in a moment I think."

"I wish this ride would last an hour," Virginia declared dreamily.

Looking down, Judy saw Miss Ward and Beverly in the chair directly beneath. After that came Ardeth and Betty, who waved and shouted something she could not hear.

Next Judy turned her attention to a distant valley. Now that the lift chair was very high, she could see the gap in the mountains which she thought must be Penguin Pass.

"Look over there," she directed Virginia's gaze. "Did you ever see anything so beautiful?"

"What's that black stuff sticking up? Or is it metal?"

"Where, Virginia?"

"Almost as far as you can see, toward Penguin Pass."

"Oh, I see it now! Why, it looks like the wreckage of a plane partially covered with snow!"

"It does, Judy."

"But how could that be?" Judy frowned as she adjusted her goggles.

"We know a plane was wrecked near Penguin Pass."

"True, but Mr. Shively told us every trace of it had been removed."

"That's so."

"It's a wreck of a plane, I'm sure," Judy announced with sudden conviction. "Virginia, seeing it there interests me tremendously! As soon as we reach the top, I mean to learn more about it!"

Chapter 15

A Severed Wire

THE ski chair came to rest with scarcely a bump. Judy slid out and helped Virginia alight.

Once they were out of the way. the next chair was brought to a halt in the same manner and Miss Ward and Beverly slid out. A moment more and they were joined by the remaining members of the party.

"Oh, that was glorious!" Miss Ward declared. "Mr. Shively was right. It is more fun here than at Maple Leaf Lodge."

"Also it gets us out of his hair," Kathleen added dryly. "Not that I don't like it here. I'm positively thrilled!"

"Where do we start on the ski trails?" Beverly asked impatiently. "No use wasting time."

Miss Ward pointed out the beginner's trail. It wound down the mountain at an easy angle, and a fall there, would not likely mean more than a few bruises.

The other two trails were so steep that with exception of Judy and Miss Ward, no member of the patrol had the skill to attempt them.

For that reason, everyone was surprised and a bit

dismayed when Beverly dug in her poles and coolly announced that she would try the most difficult of the trails.

"We'll carry you away in a stretcher if you do," Kathleen said bluntly. "Beverly, you're not serious."

"I am."

"In that case I'll have to forbid it, Beverly," Miss Ward said.

"But why? I thought we came here to ski."

"Try the easy slope first, Beverly. If you can manage that one without mishap, then we'll discuss the harder one."

Beverly accepted the order but in none too good grace. Rather indignantly, she made her way to the beginner's slope.

Confident of her ability, she started down fast without even bothering to study the terrain. Before she had made half the run, she wound up in a tangle of skis. Beverly rolled over and over before she finally came to rest against a scrub pine.

From above, the other members of the patrol who had witnessed the mishap, had difficulty controlling their laughter. Knowing that Beverly would be furious, they managed to maintain fairly serious faces.

"Are you hurt, Bev?" Ardeth called down.

"No, I'm not!" Beverly retorted, brushing snow from her clothing. "I'd like to see you do it! This slope is a lot steeper than it looks."

A Severed Wire

"I could have told you that," Ardeth remarked to herself. "But did you ask, my pretty?"

Virginia and Betty next attempted the slope, and successfully reached the bottom without a tumble. Ardeth, however, allowed her skis to get ahead of her, and ended by sliding part of the way.

As Miss Ward prepared to tackle the more difficult slope, Judy walked over to the little house where the chair lift attendant had taken refuge from the elements. He was a young man, not more than twenty-three, with a shock of sandy hair.

"Good morning," Judy said pleasantly. "You seem to be quite busy."

"Oh, we haven't too many using the lift," he replied. "On week-ends we get a crowd from the city."

"The view from the ski chair is amazing," Judy went on. She waved her hand toward the gap between the mountains, saying casually: "That, I suppose is the well known Penguin Pass."

"Right."

"Do skiers use the slopes there very much?"

"Not this winter. The ski patrol has advised against it."

"Any particular reason?"

"No, except that its a difficult area to patrol."

"There's the danger of slides too, I suppose."

"The snows are heavier there," the lift attendant agreed. "But at this time of year, we're not likely to get a slide."

Judy was tempted to tell him of the Scouts' experience the previous day, but decided against it. Time was short and she had several questions to ask. The ski chairs had started to move again, which meant that as soon as the passengers reached the top of the slope, the attendant would be busy.

"Coming up a moment ago, I saw something that looked liked wreckage buried in the snow," she remarked.

"That's what it is."

"Wreckage of a plane?"

"Right."

"But I thought—that is, wasn't it ever cleared away?"

"Nope. Still there. That's one reason the ski patrol has discouraged skiers from going near the Pass. Too many might be tempted to do a little souvenir hunting. Nothing of value left there, of course."

"It seems rather goulish to look for souvenirs from a wrecked plane."

"You'd be surprised what some folks find interesting," the attendant declared grimly. "There's one fellow in particular, who combs the area almost every day."

"Who is he?"

"I don't know or care. He never uses the lift, but comes in from the other direction. Penguin Pass is so far away, I can't make out his face, even with

A Severed Wire

binoculars. He goes there almost every day though, poking about in the wreckage."

A chair, bearing two men skiers, now had reached the top of the slope. The attendant went out to release the safety bar so that they could alight. After that, he was kept too busy to talk further with Judy.

She waited awhile, several times attempting to resume the interrupted conversation.

"If you're interested in the plane wreck, why not talk to Mr. Hawkins in Weston," the attendant advised. "He was a member of the expedition that brought out the survivors. He can tell you anything you want to know about the accident."

"Thanks, a lot," Judy said gratefully.

Mr. Hawkins, she reflected, never so much had hinted of any part in the rescue work. She made up her mind to talk to him about it whenever she returned to the Weston general store.

As she was adjusting her ski bindings, preparatory to starting down to join her friends, the chair unloaded Betty and Virginia. Beverly too had struggled up the slope, though afoot.

"Hey, chicken, how about you?" the latter demanded of Judy. "Afraid to try it?"

"Not exactly," Judy returned with a smile. "I was taking in the scenery, that's all."

"Well, expert, show us how it's done," Beverly challenged. "We're waiting. You'll try the most difficult trail, of course?"

"I'd intended to tackle the intermediate one first. But if you want to make a point of it, I'll start with the advanced and work down to my proper level."

"Let's see you make it," Beverly urged. "If you do, I'll take your place washing dishes tonight."

"It's a deal," grinned Judy. "Here I go!"

Judy projected herself to the top of the slope with her poles. A moment she poised, studying the terrain below. Then she shoved off, her skis hissing on the snow as they gathered speed. Faster! Faster!

It became a struggle to keep her knees pressed forward, her body relaxed. But she took the curves with an easy, controlled motion which was beautiful to watch. Breathless, but with every fibre alive and tingling, she reached the bottom without a fall.

She rode the ski chair back up the mountain to receive the congratulations of her friends. Beverly grudgingly conceded that she would have the dishes to do that night.

After skiing for an hour, the group gathered at Bledlow Inn for a hot lunch. By three o'clock, everyone was tired, and ready to return to Maple Leaf Lodge. The Scouts did not stop in Weston, for they were offered a ride nearly to their destination.

"No skiing for me tomorrow," declared Ardeth, ruefully massaging a tender ankle.

"You didn't sprain it, I hope," Miss Ward said.

"Oh no, but the muscle is strained a bit. I've just skied too much."

A Severed Wire

"It will do us all good to rest after such a big day," Miss Ward said. "I know I intend to spend most of tomorrow by the fire."

Transportation ended at the main road. Tumbling out of the car with their skis and poles, the girls continued afoot toward Maple Leaf Lodge. The trail which had seemed endless on the night of the Scouts' arrival now no longer daunted them. There had been no snow that day, and the path was well trampled, making walking easy.

When the girls were a quarter of the way to the lodge, they saw a man with a repair kit coming toward them.

"We must have had a visitor," Ardeth declared, the first to spy the stranger. "Maybe the electric lights have been fixed."

"I hope myself that he's the telephone company man," Miss Ward commented.

The repairman paused as he met the group of girls.

"The telephone line is okay now," he informed Miss Ward.

"Oh, fine!" she replied. "What was wrong? The line, I suppose, was broken from a heavy load of ice."

"On the contrary, it had been cut."

A stunned silence greeted this information. Then Miss Ward murmured:

"Are you sure?"

"It looked that way to me," the repairman replied. "Know of anyone who would do it?"

"Why, no. There's no one at the lodge except Mr. Shively, the caretaker. You probably met him while you were there."

"No one was around. I know Caleb Shively though. He's the last person that would cut a telephone wire. The trick must have been pulled by someone who has it in for the Scouts."

"But the line was out of order when we arrived. We're not acquainted in this area either."

"I meant the Boy Scouts," the repairman said. "We occasionally have trouble with cranks who maliciously destroy property. You'll probably have no further trouble while you're at the lodge, but it's well to be alert."

"Thank you for the warning. We'll be on the lookout."

Subdued by the information they had received, the girls had little to say as they tramped on to the lodge.

Very much to their surprise, Mr. Shively met them at the gate, having snowshoed in from the opposite direction only that moment. He carried a canvas sack which contained a bulky object.

"Goodness! What do you have?" Kathleen demand curiously. "Have you been hunting?"

"I don't hunt," Mr. Shively returned in a curt voice which discouraged further questions. He offered no explanation as to what he carried in the bag, or as to where he had been.

Miss Ward remarked that the telephone line had been repaired in his absence. She reported also that the line had been severed deliberately.

"So?" Mr. Shively inquired. "I wouldn't know anything about it."

He ended the conversation at that point by stomping off to his sanctuary, the barn.

The girls divested themselves of their ski garments and assigned themselves to various tasks which needed doing. To make certain that the telephone indeed was working again, Miss Ward called the postoffice.

"There's mail being held for us," she reported. "We can go to town for it tomorrow."

"I wish Ted would write," Judy said, frowning, as she skinned out of a slip-on sweater. "I asked him to reply immediately. Of course, he hasn't had time yet."

She presently went to her room to sew on a button which had pulled from the belt of her ski trousers. As she was working on it, Kathleen came in.

"Always busy, Judy?"

"I have to be this time, if I want to do any skiing tomorrow. This button was hanging by a single thread."

"I thought we were taking a day of rest tomorrow."

"The others are."

"You have different plans?"

Judy's face was sober as she looked up from her sewing. "That depends on Miss Ward," she said distinctly. "If she turns thumbs down, then I can't do it."

"Do what, Judy?"

"I want to investigate Penguin Pass."

"After what happened there yesterday?"

"There was no excuse for that near-accident if we'd kept closer watch of the slopes."

"The fact remains we nearly were buried by a snow slide, Judy."

"I talked with the attendant of the ski lift today about it. Kathleen, he says there is very little danger at this time of year."

"But we know—"

"There was a slide," Judy finished quietly. "My theory is that it was man-made."

"By that giant who makes huge tracks? Monstro the snowman?"

"I don't know the answer," Judy said. "I want to investigate. The safety of the patrol may depend upon what we learn."

"You're so serious, Judy."

"We're involved in something serious, I think, and through no fault of our own. The fact that the telephone wire was cut is especially disturbing."

"The repairman might have been mistaken."

A Severed Wire

"It's most unlikely. I thought myself that the wire had been cut. Furthermore, I have a suspicion who did it."

"Not—?" Kathleen hesitated to frame the name that was on her lips.

"Caleb Shively," Judy finished for her. "Yes, Kathleen, I suspect he's the culprit."

"It's fantastic!"

"Mr. Shively has a fine reputation around Weston," Judy acknowledged. "I know it seems ridiculous to distruct him, but I do. Kathleen, he wants to be rid of us. If we aren't on guard, he may attempt desperate measures."

Chapter 16

Adventure

KATHLEEN could not accept completely Judy's theory that Mr. Shively had cut the telephone wire. She pointed out that the phone had been out of order upon their arrival at Maple Leaf Lodge, which was evidence that he had not severed the line to annoy the Girl Scouts.

"I think myself that Mr. Shively only wanted to live by himself this winter," she declared. "You may be right that he cut the wire. But if he did, it must have been because he didn't want anyone bothering him."

"That doesn't make sense to me," Judy argued. "A telephone is too vital in modern living. Why, Mr. Shively needed it to order groceries for himself, and in case of an emergency. He had a very real reason for breaking off communication, but what it was I can't figure out."

"We're likely suspecting him without reason, Judy. It could have been someone else, you know. Someone who disliked him or the Scouts."

"Granted. All the same, I propose to keep my eyes open and learn everything I can."

"About Penguin Pass," Kathleen resumed the original subject of their discussion. "You're not serious about going there?"

Adventure

"I am," Judy replied soberly. "I have a hunch that there's a very simple explanation for those huge snowman footprints."

"Personally, I'm willing to let the mystery go unsolved."

"I'd never rest if I did, Kathleen. Another thing, I want to visit the wreckage of that air transport."

"But I thought—"

"All the wreckage had been removed? So did I, Kathleen, but I learned yesterday that Mr. Shively told us a downright fib about it. That's another reason I want to check up on him."

"Judy, you couldn't explore the Pass alone," Kathleen said firmly. "You're by far the best skier in the patrol, but even so, it isn't safe. You advised against it when Beverly led the patrol."

"True," Judy conceded. She sat down at the dresser, vigorously brushing her hair until it glistened like satin. "I wouldn't want to take the patrol there even now. I propose to go alone."

"You simply can't," Kathleen argued. "It's unsafe."

"I'd start early in the day and go well equipped."

"What if there should be another snowslide?"

"One would have to be alert for them," Judy said. "According to the ski lift attendant, this isn't the time slides usually start on Candy Mountain."

"One did though. And we might have been buried under it!"

"It wasn't a real avalanche, Kathleen. Besides, I

think it was touched off purposely to frighten the patrol from the trail."

"All the more reason then that we should stay away."

"And never learn the answer to our questions?"

"We-ll, it's not good Scouting to take such risks as you're proposing, Judy. Let's talk it over with Miss Ward."

"We know what she will say."

"Thumbs down. She's already advised us to stay away from Penguin Pass."

"That was because of the snow slide."

"Judy," Kathleen reminded her. "You know the Scout Law as well as I do: Rule number seven. '*A Girl Scout Obeys Orders.*'"

Judy tossed aside the hair brush with a decisive flip of the wrist. "In that case, there's only one thing to do," she announced. "The orders must be changed."

"You might try," Kathleen said. "If you get permission to go to the Pass, count me in. You'll need a buddy to look after you."

Gathering up a handful of woolen socks she meant to wash, Judy left the bedroom. She was gone a full twenty minutes. When she returned it was to find Kathleen lying relaxed and half asleep on the lower bunk.

"It's arranged, Kathy!" she announced.

Kathleen sat up. "Miss Ward gave you permission to go to Penguin Pass?"

Adventure

"She did. We start first thing after breakfast."

"We?" Kathleen asked weakly. "Say, what did I promise anyhow?"

"You don't have to do it. Anyway, Miss Ward is going along."

"Why didn't you say so?" Kathleen demanded in relief. "That's different."

"I was sort of surprised. I told Miss Ward all my reasons for wanting to investigate, and believe it or not, she didn't offer a single argument. In fact, I suspect she had been thinking along the same lines herself. She just said: 'I'll go with you.'"

"Miss Ward didn't look too well today after we got back from the inn," Kathleen remarked. "She may be coming down with a hard cold."

"Or flu. I hope not, Kathy, but she did look rather pale. Anyway, unless something goes wrong, the trip is set for tomorrow. We're not to say anything to the other Scouts though."

The next morning, Judy was the first abroad in the lodge. As she set the table in the warm kitchen, she peered through the window at a slightly overcast sky.

"It looks like snow," she thought uneasily. "I hope we don't have a storm. That would ruin all my plans."

An intensive program of skiing and hiking had tired all of the patrol members with exception of Judy, whose leg muscles had been conditioned by two weeks of hard outdoor exercise. On this particular morning, the girls arose with more reluctance than usual, and at the breakfast table announced their intentions of "taking it easy" that day.

Kathleen made no comment, but glanced at Miss Ward. The Scout leader had a slight cold and looked very tired, as if she had not slept well.

"I want to hike down to Weston for the mail," Ardeth announced. "That is, if I can make it under my own steam. Anyone want to go along?"

Virginia and Beverly volunteered, and finally Betty decided she too would make the trip. Judy, Kathleen and Miss Ward casually mentioned that they might spend the time on skis.

"You're gluttons for punishment, that's all I can say," remarked Betty. "Well, more power to you."

By ten o'clock the three had departed for Weston. A half hour later, after making careful preparation, Judy, Kathleen and Miss Ward were ready to leave the Inn.

"As a precaution, I'll leave a note for the girls, telling them where we have gone," the Scout leader said. "I hope we'll be back here ahead of the others. But if not, I don't want them to worry about our absence."

"Where's Mr. Shively this morning?" Kathleen asked, as they started off together.

"The fires were built when I awoke," Judy re-

Adventure

joined. "I haven't seen him around anywhere though. He seems to give us as wide a berth as possible."

Miss Ward let the girls set the pace. Noting that the leader seemed very tired, her movements jerky, Judy took the slopes rather slowly. However, the first steep herring-bone climb left Miss Ward quite breathless.

"I-I'm afraid I over-did yesterday," she puffed, pausing to rest. "Either that, or I'm coming down with a hard cold. I seem to be delaying the party."

"We'll have plenty of time if it doesn't snow," Judy said, studying the leaden sky. "The weather looks rather threatening."

Before long, the trio came to the trail guarded by Monstro. Wind had drifted snow into many of the huge footprints, but a few remained visible.

Judy led the way between the sentinel pines, climbing slowly to avoid exhaustion. When it became difficult to use skis, she shouldered them, deciding that they would be needed later for the descent into the hidden valley.

The closely spaced evergreens with their thickly laden branches had an eerie aspect of unreality. Long icicles clung to some of the limbs, and occasionally, as she passed, Judy would strike them off with her ski pole.

As they wound deeper into the mountain, the

trio proceeded with increasing caution. Judy and Miss Ward constantly scanned the slopes where snow lay in a heavy blanket.

Finally, Judy drew up at the point where the Scouts had been terrorized by the snowslide. The trail had not been blocked, for most of the snow had slid on into the valley.

"I'd like to climb that slope and look around," Judy said. "If the slide was started by a human being, there should be footprints to show it."

Miss Ward hesitated. "You might start another slide, Judy," she said doubtfully.

"I'll climb very slowly, and feel my way. I know it's safe, especially as most of the loose snow already has come down."

Reluctantly, the Scout leader granted permission for the climb.

Judy moved up the slope cautiously, studying the contours, and estimated from which direction a slide might come. The snow felt firm beneath her. She drew confidence, and turned to wave reassuringly to the two anxious watchers below.

Now and then she stamped hard to test the cohesion of the snow. She steadily worked her way upward, convinced that there no longer was any danger.

Before she had climbed far, Judy saw above her two of the telltale footprints which had not been obliterated.

Adventure

Directing herself toward them, she trailed them to a clump of evergreens.

So now she had the proof! The huge prints were evidence indeed that someone had hidden behind the trees two days earlier. Whether or not the snowslides had been started by accident or deliberately, she had no way of determining.

Judy searched the snow for clues which might identify the man with the monstrous footprints. She found nothing, and finally descended the slope to rejoin Miss Ward and Kathleen.

"Those footprints are unbelievable!" Miss Ward declared, leaning on her poles. "I wonder if it is wise to go on?"

"Oh, we must!" Judy urged. "We're only at the threshold, so to speak. I do so want to reach the valley beyond the Pass."

"We'll go on," Miss Ward decided. "I'll stay with you if I can."

Excitement filled Judy with a driving surge of power. She could have pushed on tirelessly at an even faster pace. But she noted that Miss Ward was falling farther and farther behind. Obviously, the leader was not well.

"Perhaps we should turn back," she conceded as she waited until Kathleen and Miss Ward came up. "The climb from here to the Pass will be even harder. After that the drop to the valley should be easy. But the way back won't be a simple matter."

"I can keep going for awhile," Miss Ward said, shivering. "I feel chilly although I dressed warmly this morning."

"You're having a chill," Kathleen said anxiously. "We should return to the lodge."

"Purely because of me?" the teacher smiled wanly. "I never dreamed I would prove to be such a softie."

"You're ill," Judy declared. "I think you're coming down with a cold."

"I am. I know it."

"There's only one place for you," Kathleen insisted. "Beside the fire, with a bowl of soup, and cold tablets."

"I'm afraid I'll have to turn back," Miss Ward decided. "It's a pity after we've come so far. Judy, do you and Kathleen think you could manage it by yourselves?"

"On to the valley?" Judy questioned eagerly.

"How long would it take?"

"That's hard to say. I'd judge we might reach the Pass in a half hour or less. The descent to the valley will be fast. The climb back necessarily will be slow."

"With luck you should be back to the lodge in three or four hours."

"Oh, before that," Judy said confidently. "You don't mind if we go on alone?"

"Yes, it worries me," Miss Ward replied. "However, this expedition is an important one. There's only one thing—"

Adventure

"Monstro?" Judy supplied.

"You're not afraid?"

"No," Judy returned soberly. "I can't believe that those footprints aren't phoney somehow. My mind tells me a giant couldn't inhabit this area."

"If you should see anyone, what would you do?"

"Run. I promise I won't try to get within a thousand yards of Monstro or any of his kin."

"And I'll see that she lives up to that promise," Kathleen declared grimly.

Miss Ward smiled, and offered Judy her ruck sack. "You'll find some sandwiches in there," she declared. "Also a hatchet, some matches, and a few odds and ends that might come in handy in case of an emergency. A flashlight too."

"We won't need a light. We'll be back long before dusk," Kathleen declared.

"You'll have it at any rate," Miss Ward said. "One never knows what can happen on a rugged trail such as this. I'd never let you go on alone, if I weren't feeling so miserable."

"Are you sure you can make it alone to the lodge?" Judy asked.

"Of course. I'm not really ill, only feeling miserable. And this rarefied air snatches my breath. You'll both be very cautious?"

Judy and Kathleen nodded.

"If the weather should turn bad, start for the lodge at once."

"We will," Judy promised.

Miss Ward began the descent. Judy and Kathleen watched her until she was lost beyond a bend in the trail. Then resolutely they turned their faces toward Penguin Pass and the adventure which awaited them.

Chapter 17

The Igloo Storehouse

THE trail dipped downward for a short distance, and then wound up the mountainside again through a sparse stand of evergreens. Kathleen and Judy climbed determinedly, seldom speaking.

Both girls were deeply impressed with the responsibility which had fallen upon them. In permitting them to go on alone, they knew that Miss Ward had placed high trust in their ability and judgment. They could not fail her!

Judy pulled the visor of her ski cap lower over her eyes. Though the sun shone only intermittently, the glare was rather annoying. She rubbed a film of moisture from her colored goggles, and then removed them completely.

Blinking in the bright light, she gazed fixedly toward a clump of snow-topped evergreens to the right of the trail.

"Look, Kathleen!" she directed.

With a mittened hand, she pointed toward a half-hidden snow hut on the mountainside. It was built of square blocks of ice and snow, and had a rounded top which partially had collapsed.

"Well, we *have* made a discovery!" Kathleen exclaimed, astonished. "Shall we climb up and look at it closely?"

Judy hesitated. Before making reply, she glanced alertly in all directions to satisfy herself that no one loitered in the area.

"Kathy, I think you should wait here on the trail," she said finally. "I'll climb up there and take a peek. It won't take long."

"Hurry," the other advised. "It's getting colder, and I'll freeze if I stand here many minutes."

"I'll be as fast as I can," Judy promised.

She climbed the steep slope and at first was reassured to note only unbroken snow, except for the telltale tracks left by her own boots. But as she went over a rise, she saw that in the vicinity of the igloo, the snow had been trampled. Approaching the snow hut from the rear were many footprints, all of them huge.

"I've found the lair of the snowman," she called down to Kathleen who watched anxiously from below.

Judy tried to make a joke of it, but actually the sight of the over-sized prints cast a pall over her. How could any man of normal proportions leave behind such monstrous tracks? Snow had blown into many of the footprints, but even this observation, brought small comfort.

Circling the snow hut, Judy peered in through the sizeable doorway. No one was there. But stashed against the back wall was a supply of canned goods.

The Igloo Storehouse

Crawling in, Judy inspected the stores. There were cans of beans, soup, corned beef hash and a dozen other items.

Before she had completed the investigation to her satisfaction, Kathleen called from the trail below.

"Hurry, Judy! I'm freezing to death!"

"Coming."

Judy crawled out and slid down the slope to rejoin her chum. There she related her astonishing discovery.

"Don't you suppose the Bledlow Ski Patrol stached the food for emergency purposes?" Kathleen speculated.

Judy had not thought of this possibility. She mulled over it for a moment and then shook her head.

"Skiers seldom use the runs in this direction, Kathy. Besides, I noticed—"

"What, Judy?"

"More of those huge footprints. This igloo must have been built by that same man or creature that left his shoeprints beside our snowman."

"I wish you wouldn't keep referring to him as a creature," Kathleen remonstrated. "It makes me nervous. I conjure up a picture of a pre-historic caveman about to pounce on me from behind an evergreen."

"It's no joking matter," Judy agreed soberly. "The

last thing I want to do is to meet the owner of those over-sized shoes. However, finding this igloo convinces me of one thing."

"What, Judy?"

"Well, we're on the trail of a real person. One who eats substantial food, and has cached a supply away for emergency use."

"It could be a ski patrol supply station."

"The ski patrol wouldn't build a snow igloo, I'm sure," Judy returned. "They'd have a more substantial shelter. The person who built this snow hut did it very recently, possibly in the last few days, and must plan to use the supplies very soon."

"Now that we've discovered this place, what?"

"We may make other discoveries before the day is over."

"Then you mean to push on?"

"Yes, I want to reach the site of the plane wreck, if possible. If you're tired, Kathy, you should turn back."

"And permit you to go on alone? Never!"

"I knew you'd say that!" Judy grinned. "Well, let's hit the trail then. Time is running out on us."

Without further adventure, the girls climbed to Penguin Pass there halting to regain their breath and to drink in an exalting view. Also, they broke into the sandwiches and cookies which Miss Ward thoughtfully had packed in her rucksack. A pint

The Igloo Storehouse

thermos bottle provided them with refreshing drinks of hot tomato soup.

"There! I feel like a million dollars now!" Judy declared, when the repast was finished. "Shall we shove on?"

"How much farther?"

"We're headed down into the valley where that wreckage can be seen," Judy said, pointing out the dark mass looming from a sea of white. "It shouldn't take long to ski down."

"But then we'll have a hard climb back," Kathleen said, drawing a deep sigh.

"True. That can't be avoided. Kathy, why not be sensible about it? You wait here for me where it's sheltered. I'll never be out of your sight."

"The slope looks so steep. If you should fall—"

"I won't," Judy said confidently. "But if I should be unlucky enough to have an accident, you'd be in better position to help me, or go for assistance. How about it?"

"All right," Kathleen reluctantly agreed. "I'll watch you from here every second. Hurry as fast as you can."

"You may be sure I will," Judy promised, adjusting her skis.

"Be careful of slides."

"Don't worry about anything, Kathleen," Judy said reassuringly. "I'll ski with brakes all the way down."

Determined to take no chances, she mapped out her descent before shoving off. Her first lap took her to a wide shelf on the slope where she brought up to study the terrain below.

She tested the snow and then went down the next slope in a movement so swift that it brought a thrill of pleasure. The final run was through evergreens where the slightest miscalculation would have resulted in a disastrous spill.

Reaching the valley floor, Judy waved reassuringly to Kathy and received an answering signal. Satisfied that all was well with her friend, she then turned her back upon Penguin Pass and glided toward the wreckage of the transport, visible six hundred yards away.

A stimulating sense of excitement made Judy unaware of the weariness of her body. The feeling that she might be on the verge of a vitally important discovery was heightened as she presently drew closer to the wreckage. In its immediate vicinity the snow had been heavily trampled. Everywhere there were huge shoeprints, and a concentration of them close to the crumbled plane.

"Monstro was here all right," Judy thought grimly.

Both wings of the wrecked transport had been sheared off by the teriffic impact. Loose items such as seats, wheels and bits of the propeller had vanished completely, evidently carried away by souvenir hunters.

The Igloo Storehouse

Judy circled the wreckage and poked about in it for a brief space. The feeling of discovery and high elation fast was fading. Save for the mysterious footprints which were everywhere, there was nothing to stir her interest. The dead wreckage answered none of her questions.

"What is there here to draw one?" she speculated. "Why should that man with the big feet come here repeatedly?"

That the one she had dubbed "Monstro" frequently had visited the site seemed fairly evident. For how otherwise, could one explain so many shoeprints? Some obviously had been made quite recently, while others were frozen over and days old.

Judy was loath to leave the area without obtaining information which would aid her in piecing together the puzzle, but she dared linger no longer. Kathleen would be waiting. Besides, the sky had taken on an ominous cast which forewarned of snow.

Abruptly turning her back upon the mass of twisted aluminum and steel, Judy studied the slopes to determine the easiest way to Penguin Pass.

As she started on again through the deep snow, her ski struck a hard, metallic object. Judy groped until she found the item.

Surprisingly, it was a jewelled cigarette case, once beautiful but now covered with a thin layer of tarnish and rust.

"Someone on the plane must have owned this," Judy thought. "In the crash it was thrown clear and souvenir hunters missed it."

She started to abandon the case to the snow, and then on impulse slipped it into the pocket of her gabardine ski trousers.

As she began the difficult climb to rejoin Kathy, the first snowflakes began to fall. Small and hard, they came steadily and with driving force. For the first time, Judy became aware that her toes tingled with cold.

"The temperautre must have dropped a lot in the last hour or so," she thought uneasily. "I hope we're not in for a hard storm."

Chapter 18

Into the Blizzard

SNOW continued to fall steadily as Judy, after an exhausting climb, finally reached Penguin Pass. Shaking the caked flakes from her neck scarf, she looked anxiously about for Kathleen.

Her chum was nowhere to be seen. Repeatedly, Judy shouted her name, but the rising wind flung back the call.

Kathleen's tracks had been all but obliterated by the blowing snow, but there were enough remaining to disclose that the girl had wandered off some distance from the point where she had been assigned to wait.

Searching, Judy ultimately sighted Kathy huddled against a rock which offered considerable protection from the bite of the wind.

"Oh, there you are!" Kathleen cried, seeing her at the same moment. She came out of the shelter. "Judy, I thought you'd never come! You've been gone hours."

"I hurried as fast as I could."

"I waited for you a while, Judy. Then I began to get cold, so I crawled under that rock. Any luck? What did you learn?"

Judy briefly reported finding the same over-sized

shoe tracks in the immediate vicinity of the airplane wreckage.

"I picked this up too," she said, displaying the rusty jeweled cigarette case.

Kathy glanced at the item with a flash of curiosity, fingering it a moment, and noting that it was empty except for a couple of stained cigarettes. Her interest, however, was short lived.

"Judy, this storm is getting very bad," she said. "We must start for the lodge at once. I'm sort of scared."

"Scared? Why?"

"Before the snow closed in, I could see the ski lift from here. It's stopped running."

"That's customary in any snow storm."

"Even the ski patrol has returned to Bledlow Inn," Kathleen resumed, her teeth chatting. "There was a long line of men, Judy. From here, they resembled a parade of tiny, black ants going down the mountainside. After they left, the lift ceased operation."

"The snow is coming down fast and hard," Judy acknowledged. "We'll make it all right though. Going back should be easier, because we'll be running downhill more of the time."

"The wind is rising—"

"We're in an exposed position here at the Pass," Judy said, deliberately cheerful. "There's no time to lose though. Ready?"

Kathleen made a final check of her ski bindings, and nodded.

Into the Blizzard

Judy went ahead, lowering her head against the force of the wind. No matter how she took the slopes, she seemed always to be boring directly into it. Snow came from everywhere, driving into her face and lashing her cheeks.

"This is no ordinary snow storm," Judy thought with mounting uneasiness. "It's the start of a blizzard."

As fear chilled her, she instinctively quickened her pace, crouching lower to gain more momentum. When she looked back, Kathleen was far behind, nearly blotted out by the blanket of snow.

Judy waited for her chum to come up. Kathleen stopped beside her with an awkward movement of her skis.

"Don't get so far ahead of me, Judy," she gasped. "I can't go as fast as you. I—I nearly lost you twice."

"I'll go slower," Judy promised. "I didn't realize I was so far ahead. We don't dare waste any time though."

"This driving snow is horrible, and it's getting worse!"

"It is!" Judy acknowledged. "They'll be worried about us at the lodge. All the more reason why we can't delay."

"It's so hard to see ahead, Judy, are you sure of the way?"

"If it doesn't get worse, we'll be all right. I have my compass."

They shoved off again, this time keeping as close together as possible. The wind screamed in their faces and all but tore them apart when they passed beyond the partial shelter of rock ledges and towering trees. Snow which came down unbelievably fast, lashed their faces and caked their goggles so that they could not see.

They swooped down another slope and then began the more tortuous part of the homeward trip. The wind now penetrated their clothing, and fingers which gripped ski poles became numb with cold.

Judy had lost all knowledge of time, for she had neglected to wind her wristwatch that morning. She knew though, that it was well past mid-afternoon. The sky was darkening, almost as if twilight were coming on.

Her knees were trembling, as she poled off again. The long climb from the valley to Penguin had tired her more than she liked to acknowledge. It seemed to take her last iota of strength to keep boring into the teeth of the gale.

With the shriek of wind in her ears, she negotiated the wooded trail. Her tired knees absorbed the shock as she bounced over rough terrain. A small rock, hidden from her view by the blinding snow, loomed up. Instinctively, she leaped it, and tried to shout a warning to Kathleen who was close behind.

But the wind snatched her words and flung them away.

Into the Blizzard

Kathleen failed to see the rock until it was too late to avoid it. She swerved, missing the boulder by inches, but brought up with a splintering of wood on another projection.

"Are you hurt?" Judy shouted anxiously.

Receiving no reply, she climbed back and tried to help Kathy to her feet. But her friend resisted her efforts, whimpering piteously.

"Get up, Kathy. You must!"

"I can't. It's my ankle. I think I've broken it."

"Nonsense," Judy said brusquely. "It was only a little spill. Try to get onto your feet. Lean on me."

Kathleen made an effort, only to collapse again in the snow.

"I simply can't, Judy. It's broken."

A great fear had gripped Judy, but she dared not show her real feeling, lest she increase Kathy's panic. Their plight which before had been serious, now was almost desperate.

One of Kathy's skis had been shattered. As if that were not bad enough, Kathy's injured ankle might make it impossible for them to proceed. And yet they didn't dare remain where they were. The temperature steadily was falling, and the snow showed not the slightest indication of letting up. Why, the blizzard might last another twenty-four hours or longer! By that time—

Judy ripped off her mittens to examine Kathy's ankle. She could feel no broken bones, though her chum moaned with pain at the slightest touch.

"It's a bad sprain, I think," Judy said. "Kathy, I know I'm asking a lot, but we're in a bad spot. You'll have to try to go on. I'll help you."

"I'll try," Kathy promised, biting her lower lip to keep back the tears.

After two attempts, Judy succeeded in getting Kathleen on her feet. But she could not take a single step forward without writhing in pain.

"I can't make it, Judy. You'll have to go on without me and bring help."

Judy considered briefly and shook her head. She didn't dare leave Kathy alone even for an hour. In her weakened condition, she might freeze to death.

"If only we could get to that igloo we'd have shelter at least," she said, thinking aloud. "It can't be much farther on."

"I never can make it, Judy. Every step kills me. Just let me stay here."

"No! There must be some way. Let me think—"

"If we had some cord, you might make a toboggan of our skis, Judy. You didn't bring a rope?"

"It's about the only thing I left behind. There may be one in Miss Ward's rucksack."

Judy poked into it but though the teacher had included many useful articles, there was no rope or cord.

"I know!" Judy muttered. "I'll use the laces of my ski boots."

Into the Blizzard

"Not yours—mine." Kathleen advised. "I can't use my boots, while yours are vitally important. Even if you can make the toboggan, can you pull me in this dreadful storm?"

"I can and I will."

Advised by Kathleen, Judy set about trying to make a sled of the three good skis and the one which had been splintered at its end. First she laid them side by side, the tips even.

With the hatchet Miss Ward had included in the rucksack, she cut two crude crosspieces from a bare tree branch. The first she lashed across the bow of the four skis, and fastened the second to the ski bindings.

"That's the best I can do without rope," she said anxiously. "I can't tie you to the toboggan, Kathy. Do you think you can stick on?"

"I can and will," Kathleen replied, using Judy's own phrase.

The skis made a fairly satisfactory sled, but to pull Kathleen was a task almost beyond Judy's strength. The inclines were most exhausting, and going down the slope, she experienced great difficulty in keeping her patient on the improvised toboggan.

Judy's breathing came harder and harder. The wind seemed to take fiendish delight in holding her back and its sting brought tears to her eyes. She realized that she was making slower and slower progress. How much longer could she keep on?

The Girl Scouts at Penguin Pass

When it seemed to her that she could not trudge another step, her heart leaped with hope. Through the wall of falling snow, evergreens and other landmarks suddenly were familiar. She had reached the point in the trail where the storehouse igloo had been built!

In the swirling, blowing snow, Judy could not see far ahead. But as surely as if it had loomed before her, she was certain that the igloo was on the slope above the trail. If only she could pull Kathleen up the steep incline, they would have temporary shelter.

"It's my only chance." she reasoned. "I can't go on much farther—can't possibly reach the lodge. Our only hope is to hole in and wait for help."

Chapter 19

Shelter

GASPING and panting, Judy dragged the crude toboggan up the slope through the deep drifts. Her fingers now were so nearly frozen that she scarcely could hold to the ski pole which served as a means of pulling the sled.

But the igloo rose before her to spur her to greater effort. She would make it! She had to make it!

In the end, she abandoned the toboggan and half carried Kathleen the few remaining feet to the shelter. Once there they crawled in and collapsed on the snowy floor.

Her breath recovered, Judy aroused herself sharply. Though the snow hut provided some protection from the bitter wind and the cold, snow kept drifting down upon them from a break in the roof. Kathleen was uttering no complaint, but her face was pale and her lips blue.

"If only we had a fire—" Judy murmured.

The rucksack had been abandoned with the toboggan. There was no wood.

"Might as well wish for the moon," Kathleen chattered.

"Wait here," Judy said. "I'll see what I can scare up."

"I'm not going anywhere" Kathy muttered with a wan smile. "But don't go far, Judy. In this blizzard, you could easily lose your way."

"I'll be right back. Keep up your courage."

Driving herself out into the swirling snow, Judy recovered the rucksack. The wind snatched her breath and screamed in her ears.

Fighting her way back toward the igloo, Judy searched desperately for anything that would burn. She found a few dead branches, moist from snow, but nothing more. Discouraged, she carried the salvage back to the igloo.

"Judy, beyond the stores of canned goods, I discovered a gunny sack!" Kathleen greeted her. "Guess what? A little kindling wood. And it's dry!"

"That should help for awhile," Judy said. "Providing I can get a fire started. It won't be easy."

"Build it in front of the doorway," Kathleen instructed. "That way, it will warm our hut, without melting it."

"I doubt I can get a flame with the wind blowing. But I'll try."

Judy dug down through the snow until she reached bare ground. She laid her kindling carefully, building up a snow wall to shelter it from the wind. Miss Ward had supplied a generous sized waterproof container of matches. It was well she had, for time after time, Judy failed to get her fire started. Finally, a tiny flame caught, and she nursed it faithfully, until the wood burned steadily.

The fire, small as it was, soon brought a delightful warmth to the little hut. Judy, however, dared not relax her efforts. She had to keep feeding the fire lest it smolder out. The kindling would not last long, and it was hard to make the other wood burn.

"Chop up the skis," Kathleen advised.

"Only if we're desperate," Judy decided. "I may need them again either for a toboggan or to bring help to you."

"Don't even think of leaving me," Kathleen pleaded. "Please, Judy, promise you won't. This is a dreadful storm. You might lose your way. And if I were left alone, I'd soon freeze."

"I won't leave you," Judy promised. "Keep up your courage, Kathy. Miss Ward will get help to us."

"You really think so? In this storm?"

"Yes, I do."

"But she was ill when she left us."

"Even so, she won't forget us, Kathy. Help will come."

"I think so too," Kathleen murmured drowsily. "I'm going to sleep now. That way my ankle doesn't pain me as much."

For a long while, she lay very still, but she did not sleep.

Judy divided her time between nursing the fire

and examining the stores in the igloo. There was ample food in tins, and whoever had stocked the winter hut, had thoughtfully provided a can opener.

"All the comforts of home," Judy chuckled. "Kathy, this can opener isn't even rusty. Know what that means?"

Kathy did not answer, if indeed she heard.

"All these stores must have been brought here in recent days or weeks. Otherwise, this can opener would have been rusted and useless."

Judy selected a can of beans, and getting the cover off, heated it over the fire.

"Eat this," she directed, arousing Kathy from the lethargy into which she had fallen. "It will give you strength."

Kathleen sat up and ate the hot food. Considerably cheered, she declared that her foot hurt less. Judy by this time, had ascertained to her own satisfaction that the ankle was not broken, only severely sprained. With the first-aid bandages Miss Ward had included in the rucksack, she wrapped the foot

"We're cozy and warm now, Kathy," she remarked. "But our fire can't last long. I must see if I can rustle wood. If not, our skis must be consigned to the flames."

"Don't be gone long," Kathleen said nervously. "I get sort of panicky when I'm alone here."

"I'll be back just as fast as I can."

Judy crawled out of the warm shelter into the

biting snow again. It seemed to her that the wind had dropped a trifle. At least, she felt the cold less and the snow appeared to be coming straighter down rather than at such a sharp angle.

Desperately, she searched for wood, finding few branches which offered even slight hope of catching fire.

"We're in a bad way unless help comes soon," she thought. "I'd try to make it to the lodge, if I dared leave Kathy alone."

Her eyes swept the trail, trying to pierce the curtain of snow. She stood there a moment, and then began to work her way back toward the igloo.

Suddenly, she halted. Had she heard a voice shouting from a distance, or was it merely a cruel trick of the wind. She could see no one, yet she had a strong feeling that help was near.

Cupping her hands to her lips, she warbled "Wahoo!"

The wind hurled the cry back, or was there an answering shout? Judy was afraid to hope. Nevertheless, she repeated the shout.

This time, she was certain that it was not her own voice which echoed back. From far down the trail, there was a faint, answering cry.

"Here we are! Here we are!" Judy shouted.

In her excitement, she stumbled as she sought to slide down the steep inclines to the trail below.

Moments passed and then from around a bend,

five ghost-like figures came single file. Rescue was at hand!

Judy's first thought was that Miss Ward and the Scouts had come to their aid. But as the five drew closer, she recognized the orange parkas which marked members of the mountain ski patrol.

Almost crying, so intense was her relief, Judy stumbled down the trail to meet the men. She haltingly told of Kathleen's accident and directed the rescue party to the igloo on the slope.

"We'll get her right out," one of the ski patrol men assured her. "You were smart to seek shelter instead of trying to fight the blizzard."

The men wrapped Kathleen in blankets, preparatory to taking her down from the mountain on their own sled. One of the patrol members was assigned to go ahead with Judy.

"I don't like to leave Kathy," she protested.

"She'll be well cared for now," the man assured her. "You'll help more by going on ahead."

With an expert skier breaking the trail and the wind, Judy found the going less rugged. But even so, she was grateful for an assisting arm on the last lap of the trip to Maple Leaf Lodge.

As the pair stumbled up the shoveled path to the dwelling, the door was flung open by Ardeth. Never had a fire looked so wonderful as the one which roared in the lodge room.

The Scouts peeled off Judy's outer clothing for

Shelter

her, and rubbed her icy hands. Both she and her rescuer were plied with a multitude of questions. Judy answered them as best she could.

Miss Ward, suffering from a headcold, had arisen from the bed to take command of rescue operations.

"As soon as I left you and Kathleen on the mountain, I felt I had made a grave mistake," she declared. "I never should have done it, but at the moment I was so miserable, I apparently didn't think clearly."

"After returning here, I went directly to bed. I must have slept hard, because I never awakened until Virginia pounded on the door of my room."

"I was worried about you and Kathleen," Virginia explained. "You were gone so long, and the storm began so suddenly and so hard."

"The moment I looked out the window, I realized that we were in a blizzard." Miss Ward resumed. "I wanted to start out to search for you at once. The girls felt I wasn't able. We asked Mr. Shively to help us—"

"He refused," Virginia interposed indignantly. "Can you believe it? He said he wouldn't venture a step into such a severe storm!"

"Where is he now?" Judy asked.

"Either in his room or at the barn. He gives us a wide berth, and he'd better too!"

"I did what I thought was the wisest thing," Miss Ward continued. "I telephoned the ski patrol at Bledlow Inn. Four very able men came here at once. I'd have gone with them, but they convinced me they could travel much faster alone. I only hope and pray that Kathleen will be brought in safely."

"She will be," said the young man, who had rescued Judy. He unzipped his orange parka and stretched his long legs by the fire. "The blizzard is letting up. They'll be bringing her in any minute now."

The quiet confidence of the skier whose name was Frank Ludwig, proved contagious. Forgetting their fears for Kathleen, the girls moved quickly and quietly about, preparing a room.

"The one she has shared with Judy is too cold for an invalid," Miss Ward decided. "We'll make up a bed adjoining Mr. Shively's quarters above the kitchen. Both those rooms absorb more heat from downstairs."

By the time everything was in readiness, Judy glimpsed the four ski patrol members trudging toward the lodge, pulling the sled.

"Here they come!" she cried, laughing aloud in her relief.

Kathleen, who seemed amazingly strong and cheerful, despite her misadventure, was carried by the skiers to the upstairs bedroom. There, one of the patrol members, a young doctor named Elkin Jones, examined Kathleen's ankle. He confirmed

Shelter

that it was only a bad sprain, not a break.

"No more skiing for a few days," he ordered. "Keep her in bed and she'll be all right."

Kathleen was too weary to protest the order which would rob her of fun while at Maple Leaf Lodge. She murmured her gratitude to her rescuers, and then snuggling down into the blankets, went instantly off to sleep.

The five ski patrol members drank hot coffee in the lodge kitchen before starting back to Bledlow Inn. By this time the wind had dropped somewhat but driving conditions remained hazardous. The skiers had left their car at the main highway.

"The snow should let up by tomorrow at least," Dr. Jones told Miss Ward. "You'll still have a few days to get in some good skiing before your vacation is over."

"After what happened today?"

"Accidents can't be helped," the doctor said cheerfully "Skiing is a wonderful sport. I'd advise though, that your girls remain on the easier trails. Penguin Pass is only for the experts."

"I never intend to go there again," Judy asserted earnestly.

"It's odd that Caleb Shively wouldn't help," Frank Ludwig remarked as the five men prepared to depart. "We've always depended on him in an emergency. Once when a couple of Boy Scouts were lost on the mountain, he brought them out almost on his own back. He knows this mountain like a book."

"I guess Mr. Shively likes Boy Scouts better than Girl Scouts," Ardeth remarked a trifle bitterly. "He's been most uncooperative."

The door closed behind the skiers and the girls were left to themselves. Now that the excitement was over, they urged Miss Ward to return to her bed.

"I believe I will," she consented. "If I nurse this cold, I may feel more like myself again by tomorrow."

In the doorway, Miss Ward paused to wave an admonishing finger at Judy.

"No more adventures," she scolded mildly. "Penguin Pass must be written off as a mistake."

"Not entirely," Judy grinned. She fished in her pocket and brought out the rusted cigarette case. "At least I'll have this as a souvenir of my efforts. Furthermore, I satisfied myself that Mr. Shively told us a downright falsehood about the wreckage of that transport having been removed. I think—"

She did not continue, for Ardeth raised her hand in warning. Only then did Judy hear the creak of stairsteps.

Turning around, she saw Mr. Shively coming slowly down from his bedroom. He paused to stare at the group clustered about the fireplace. His gaze then roved on and came to focus upon the jewelled case in Judy's hand.

Chapter 20

Another Loss

THE Scouts, indignant because Mr. Shively had refused to assist with the rescue of Judy and Kathleen, were inclined to treat him coldly.

"Excuse me, I think I'll run up to see how Kathleen is sleeping," Ardeth said, getting up abruptly.

"I have some work in the kitchen," Beverly announced.

If Mr. Shively knew he was being snubbed, he did not disclose it. Moving on down the stairway with cat-like tread, he came over to where Judy sat cross-legged before the crackling fire.

"What's that?" he demanded, pointing to the cigarette case she had just displayed to her friends.

"I picked it up near the wrecked plane," Judy replied. She gazed steadily at the caretaker but did not remind him in words of the falsehood he had told.

Mr. Shively took the case from Judy's hand, turning it over and over. He was smiling.

"The case seems to interest you," Judy commented.

"It is an odd souvenir. Where did you find it?"

"In the snow, not far from the wreckage."

"I suppose it belonged to some unfortunate passenger," Virginia remarked with a shudder. "Judy, you don't propose to keep it, do you?"

"I may."

"I'm not superstitious," Virginia declared, "but to me, it seems rather like a bad-luck omen. I wish you'd dispose of it, Judy."

"I'll throw it away for you," Mr. Shively offered, pocketing the case.

"No, thanks," Judy said, extending her hand. "I went through considerable to reach the valley. If it's all the same to you, I'll keep the case."

"What do you want it for?" Mr. Shively asked contemptuously. "It's no good."

"All the same, I want it." Again, she extended her hand.

Reluctantly, Mr. Shively relinquished the tarnished case. Seemingly made aware of the group's low esteem of him, he soon left the lodge and was observed enroute to his favorite haunt, the barn.

"I didn't really care much whether or not I kept the case." Judy admitted after the caretaker had gone. "I didn't want him to have it, that was all. I'm a regular dog-in-the-manger, I guess."

"Mr. Caleb Shively deserves no favors from us," Betty Bache spoke up. "He's done everything to make our stay here unpleasant."

The girls ate a light supper, carrying warm food to Kathleen and Miss Ward. Both were in an im-

Another Loss

proved condition, so it was deemed unnecessary to summon a doctor from the village.

"The snow is much lighter now and the wind is dropping," Judy informed the two patients. "I'm sure the worst of the blizzard is over."

After such a harrowing day, all the Scouts welcomed an early bed hour. Judy missed Kathleen as a roommate but agreed that she would be more comfortable in the room close to the kitchen.

"If you need anything in the night, call," she directed. "Or thump on a wall."

"All I need is sleep," Kathleen mumbled.

Judy carried the cigarette case with her to her room when she retired for the night. She dropped it on the dresser before leaping into her bunk.

Sunshine was streaming into the room, when Judy again opened her eyes. For a long while, she lay staring at the beamed ceiling, speculating upon what time it might be.

"I've overslept," she thought.

As she yawned and stretched, there came a light tap on the door. Betty came in, her shoes squeaking on the bare floor.

"What time is it?" Judy asked, arousing herself.

"About ten."

"Ten! Ye Gods and little fishes! Why didn't someone awaken me?"

"Miss Ward said to let you sleep. You needed it."

"I did!" Judy agreed, scrambling out of bed. "But I can whip my weight in mountain lions now! How are Kathleen and Miss Ward?"

"Miss Ward says she's fine. She's up and around."

"And Kathy?"

"She's better too, but Miss Ward wants her to stay in bed today, at least until after the village doctor checks her ankle."

Judy had donned a warm robe and was combing her hair vigorously. As she put the comb back on the dresser, she noticed that the jewelled cigarette case was missing.

"Betty, you didn't pick it up?" she inquired.

"Pick up what?"

"That rusty cigarette case. I left it on the dresser last night when I went to bed."

"No one has been in your room since, Judy. I'm the first one to come up here."

"You probably dropped it in the living room."

"I'm sure I didn't. Betty, we never did find that picture album that vanished."

"It was misplaced, I think," Betty reasoned. "For that matter, who would want that rusty old case? It had no value."

Judy searched the room as she dressed, but the missing case could not be found. Nor was it anywhere downstairs.

The lodge had been fairly mounded in with snow during the night and a great weight of it clung to

Another Loss

the roof. However, the blizzard had played itself out during the night and the temperature slowly was rising.

The Scouts themselves were compelled to shovel paths, for Mr. Shively had not been seen that morning.

Judy spent an hour with Kathleen, and then after an early luncheon, requested premission to go to Weston for mail and a few essential supplies. Virginia elected to accompany her.

They skied much of the way, arriving at the village in very good time. First they called at the doctor's office to deliver a message from Miss Ward, asking him to call at the lodge as soon as he conveniently could.

That errand accomplished, Virginia went to collect the mail, while Judy engaged Mr. Hawkins in talk. After making a few minor purchases, she brought up the topic of the wreck of the air transport.

"Heard about it," the storekeeper replied dryly. "Doc Jones of the Ski Patrol told around that you were a mighty plucky little girl, sticking with your friend and hauling her to the shelter after she sprained her ankle."

"Oh, that wasn't much," Judy said, flushing. "Any Scout would have done the same. Besides, the storm had started to let up, only we didn't know it. I had visions of it lasting for days!"

"Lucky for you it didn't. Whatever took you to Penguin Pass?"

"Curiosity. Mr. Hawkins, I wish you'd tell me everything you know about that plane accident. You were a member of the rescue expedition, I understand."

"Yep, I was one of a party of twenty that had to bring out the survivors and the bodies. It was a mighty gruesome experience, and I don't like to talk about it."

"I can understand that. There's just one question I want to ask, Mr. Hawkins."

"Go ahead."

"It's true, isn't it, that one of the passengers of that ill-fated plane vanished, and the body never was found?"

"Yes, it's so. An investigation was made, but no trace of the fellow ever was found."

"Who was he, Mr. Hawkins?"

"Don't recollect that I ever heard his name. He was a criminal—leastwise a man that had been arrested as a suspected spy. A Federal Bureau of Investigation man was returning him to Washington for questioning before an investigating committee when the plane crashed. The FBI man was among those killed."

"And what became of his prisoner?"

"No one knows. Some think he escaped. If he did,

Another Loss

you kin be sure he's across the border and out of the country by this time."

Virginia came up just then with an armload of mail. Before the girls had time to examine it, Mr. Hawkins offered to drive them up the mountain in his sled. Accepting the invitation gratefully, they rode as far as the private road to the lodge, there bidding him goodbye.

Entering the lodge by the rear door, the two girls found the dwelling strangely quiet. They were about to remark upon it, when they heard someone at the telephone in a room adjoining the kitchen. It was Caleb Shively's voice, and he was speaking hurriedly and in muffled tones.

"All set now—" Judy caught the words. "Meet me at Bledlow Inn. Seven tonight—sharp." Then the receiver clicked.

Chapter 21

A Missing Item

WITHOUT appearing to notice the arrival of Judy and Virginia, Mr. Shively brushed past them and went outside. From the window they saw him going directly to the barn.

"I'd like to know why he heads for the stable so often," Virginia remarked. "His devotion to that old horse is amazing."

"He was talking to someone on the 'phone when we came in," Judy said thoughtfully, stripping off her wet mittens. "He said something about everything being 'set', whatever that means."

"And that he'd meet a party at Bledlow Inn, seven sharp."

"I wonder where everyone is, Judy? The lodge is so quiet."

"Out skiing probably. Let's run up and see how Kathleen is, shall we?"

Divesting themselves of their heavy garments, they clattered up the stairway to the bedroom almost directly above the kitchen. Kathleen had propped herself to a sitting position in bed, and her eyes were alert and bright.

"Oh, I'm so glad you girls came!" she gasped in relief.

"You're here in the lodge alone?" Virginia asked.

A Missing Item

"No one to wait on you?"

"Oh, that doesn't matter. Miss Ward and the girls went out for a breath of air. I made them all go. That's not it."

"What is wrong?" Judy inquired, going to Kathy's bedside. "Do you feel well?"

"Oh, fine," Kathleen cried impatiently. "If it weren't for this stupid ankle I'd be out of here in a flash! Judy, I'm sort of scared."

"Scared? About what?"

"Mr. Shively." Kathleen lowered her voice to nearly a whisper. "Is he here in the lodge now?"

"No, he went out a moment ago, after making a 'phone call," Judy answered.

"You know his room is next to this one," Kathleen went on hurriedly. "I was lying here, sort of dozing, when I noticed that I could see his bedroom window on this side of the lodge."

"Yes?" Judy demanded quickly.

"He came to the window and opened it. Then he fished something out of the eavestrough."

"The eavestrough?" Viringia echoed. "Are you sure, Kathleen?"

"Yes, it was something hidden under the snow. The item was small and from here it appeared to be metal."

"Not a revolver?" Judy questioned.

"I don't think so. It was too small for that. I wouldn't have been frightened, only his actions were strange. He kept glancing toward my window. as if afraid he might be seen. Naturally, I pretended to be asleep."

"That Mr. Shively bears investigation," Virginia declared. "If only we dared—"

"I've been hearing odd noises from his room the last twenty minutes," Kathleen went on. "It sounded as if he were packing up to leave."

"Let's find out," Judy proposed. "Come on, Virginia."

"Be careful," Kathleen warned nervously. "Mr. Shively's the type that would be furious if he knew we were checking on him."

Their minds made up, Judy and Virginia went quickly to Mr. Shively's room adjoining. The door was closed but it was not locked.

Judy shoved it open to reveal a distressing litter. The bed apparently had not been remade in days. Furniture was covered with a layer of dust, and cobwebs festooned the pictures.

"What a mess!" Virginia said in distaste.

Judy went directly to the window. She could see where the eavestrough had been scooped clean of snow within reach from the bedroom. Kathy had been right! Mr. Shively had removed something from the trough.

"Judy! See what I've found!"

Kathleen had been examining a pile of folded clothing on the dresser. She held up the missing Boy Scout album.

A Missing Item

"So that's what became of it!" Judy cried. "And what a fuss Mr. Shively made about its disappearance!"

"All the while, he had it! Why, such a low, mean trick!"

"There must be more to it that sheer meanness, Virginia. Mr. Shively had some reason for not wanting us to examine that album. Let me see it."

Together the girls poured over the photographs, rapidly turning the pages. Suddenly, Judy was struck by thought.

"Virginia, doesn't it strike you as odd that in this entire album, there's not a single picture of Mr. Shively?"

"Well, I hadn't given it any consideration."

"Scouts taking pictures left and right, would be almost certain to include the caretaker in some of them."

"One would think so. He's very unfriendly though, and they may not have liked him very well."

"On the contrary, I remember Ted wrote that Caleb was quite jolly and popular with the boys. Another thing. Virginia, there are any number of snaps of the boys with an elderly looking man, who might have been Caleb."

"You're suggesting—"

"That it's just possible this man we've assumed to be the caretaker is only an impersonator!"

"But that's fantastic, Judy. If he isn't Caleb, where is the real caretaker?"

"I don't know. My theory may be wild, but I'm certain things aren't right here. Nothing fits into the picture the way Ted gave it to me. If only he'd answer my letter—"

"You did get one today from someone," Virginia said. "Didn't you open it?"

"I didn't even see it."

"I put all the mail in one pile on the kitchen table."

"There's only one reason why Shively would take the photograph album," Judy reverted to the original subject. "He was afraid we'd learn something about him from these pictures, and he intended to take no chances."

"It does look that way."

Now thoroughly suspicious, the girls rapidly and systematically searched the bedroom. Mr. Shively, it seemed, had few posessions. They found a suit of clothes, badly torn but all other garments were of different size and they decided, might have been borrowed or appropriated.

Then, in lifting up a pile of handkerchiefs, Judy came upon the lost cigarette case.

"Well, this is the last straw!" she exclaimed. "Our Mr. Shively is a petty thief to say the least! I suspect though, that he's no insignificant criminal. Mr. Hawkins told me this afternoon—"

Judy's final words died in her throat. The door behind her had opened softly. There on the threshold, his face ugly to behold, stood Caleb Shively!

Chapter 22

Discovery

MR. SHIVELY'S cool smile all but sent Judy and Virginia into panic. He was gazing fixedly at the rusty cigarette case.

"If you please—" he requested, extending his hand to take it.

Judy, however, had no intention of giving up the case.

"I'm sorry," she said firmly. "No doubt we owe you an apology for being here, but it seems our search has established a few rather important points. As you can see, we found the missing photograph album and this case, which in the absence of the owner, I claim."

"It must have some real value or you wouldn't have taken it!" Virginia blurted out accusingly.

Again Mr. Shively fixed her with an arrogant, insolent smile.

"You're annoying little brats," he said. "Both of you! The entire troop! But you did me a favor in finding that cigarette case. Now, if you'll be so good as to hand it over, Miss Judy Grant."

"Never!"

"Then I'll take it."

In a movement so swift that Judy was caught

completely off guard, the man leaped forward, and with a hard twist of her wrist forced her to relinquish the rusty metal case.

"Why, you monster!" Virginia shouted. "How dare you?"

In a fury, she flung herself at the man. With a mocking laugh, he seized her in a judo hold, flipping her over his back onto the floor. The next instant he was out the door, and the girls heard the key turn in the lock.

"Virginia! You're hurt!" Judy ran to help her from the floor.

"No, but I'm boiling mad! Are we locked in?"

Judy rushed to the door and twisted the handle. "We are!"

"And no one in the house except Kathleen who is bedfast!"

"Miss Ward and the others should be coming soon. It's beginning to grow dusk."

"That man should be arrested!" Virginia stormed. "I'll have him put in jail if I have to swear out the warrant myself."

"Take it easy, Virginia," Judy advised. "We're lucky things aren't much worse. I'm sure now that we were up against a desperate criminal. The worst of it is, he has what he wants now, and he may get away before we can call the authorities."

"If only Kathy could let us out of here!"

Through the thin walls, the two girls tried

Discovery

calling to their friend. Kathleen, from her bed, had heard the commotion, and was frightened half out of her wits.

"If you used a chair as a crutch, could you hobble to the door?" Judy asked.

"It's no use," Kathleen answered despairingly. "My door is locked too. I heard that villain turn the key just before he ran on down the stairway."

"Then we're stuck here until Miss Ward and the girls come," Virginia asserted. "What miserable luck."

Judy had gone to the window to gaze out across the slopes. She could see the man they knew only as Mr. Shively, skiing toward the road. But there was no evidence of Miss Ward or any of the Scouts.

"He's heading for Bledlow Inn to meet someone who will help him get away," she declared. "If only we were out of here now, we could take a short-cut trail perhaps, and get there first."

"We're not out of here," Virginia reminded her chum bitterly. "Any chance of dropping from the window?"

"Not unless we want to break our legs."

"Maybe we could tie sheets together."

"It's a long distance to the ground," Judy said dubiously. She estimated the drop, and shook her head.

"Say, they're coming!" Virginia suddenly shouted. Standing behind Judy at the window, she had caught a glimpse of skiers on a distant slope. The group definitely was moving toward the lodge.

It seemed to take hours before Judy and Virginia could distinguish faces. Finally, Miss Ward and Beverly were close enough for the girls to open the window and shout to them. Even then, they could not make their plight known, for their voices did not carry clearly.

Nevertheless, those approaching from the slopes could perceive that something was wrong. Miss Ward and Beverly started to run, Ardeth and Beverly directly behind them.

A minute or two later, they reached the lodge and came racing up the stairway.

"Is Kathleen worse?" the Scout leader called.

She went first to Kathleen's room, only to find it locked. The key, however, was in the lock, so she was able to open the door.

Kathleen quickly told of the plight of Judy and Virginia in the next room. Miss Ward immediately released them. She listened in sheer amazement as the two girls excitedly revealed what had happened.

"Mr. Shively must be an imposter!" the Scout leader cried. "I can't believe the Scout organization would employ a man of his character without learning of it! But who can this fellow be?"

"I suspect he's a wanted criminal who escaped when the plane crashed at Penguin Pass," Judy disclosed. "Mr. Hawkins was telling me about it today.

Discovery

If Ted would only answer my letter, some of this mystery might be straightened out."

"Maybe the letter is in that pile of mail I brought!" Virginia exclaimed.

With exception of Kathleen who could not leave her bed, the others rushed down to the lounge room.

"Yes, it is a letter from Ted!" Judy cried, as she rapidly ran through the mail.

Ripping open the letter, she scanned it hastily. A snapshot slipped from between the folded sheets, falling to the floor. Betty picked it up.

"What's this?" she questioned.

"A picture of my brother and some of his friends," Judy answered, for she had obtained the information from the letter. "The man with them is the caretaker."

All of the Scouts had clustered behind Betty to stare at the picture.

"The caretaker!" Beverly exclaimed. "Why, that's not Caleb Shively!"

The snapshot showed a group of Boy Scouts on the rear porch of the lodge. Ted had his hand placed affectionately on the shoulder of a middle-aged man who bore not the slightest resemblance to the caretaker known to the girls.

"This is the real Caleb," Judy said. "We have our proof now. That man who has been living here must be the man wanted by the FBI."

"We must stop him from getting away!" Miss

Ward said, starting for the telephone. "How long has he been gone, Judy?"

"Not more than ten minutes. I think he was heading for Bledlow Inn to meet someone at seven o'clock."

Miss Ward went to the wall telephone, and tried repeatedly to obtain a connection. The line was completely dead.

"Cut!" she cried despairingly. "He's severed the wire to prevent us from sounding an alert!"

Chapter 23

The Pursuit

BY examining the telephone wires outside, the Scouts quickly confirmed that the line indeed had been cut. They were convinced too, that the one they called Mr. Shively had snipped the wire on the previous occasion before their arrival, evidently hoping to isolate himself at the lodge.

"That masquerader escaped detection because no one came here who knew him," Betty declared. "He avoided telephone conversations. He never went to Weston and he hid out whenever anyone stopped here who might have become suspicious."

"What ought we to do now?" Beverly asked, turning to Miss Ward.

"It's our duty to get word to the authorities if we can."

"We'll have to hike to Weston then."

"Our fugitive is heading for Bledlow Inn," Judy pointed out. "We might get there before he leaves, by taking a short-cut trail. Instead of going down the mountain, as he is doing, why not make a sharp, hard climb to the ski lift? Then descend to the Inn."

"That would be shorter," Miss Ward agreed. "But could we make it quickly enough? And will the ski chairs still be operating?"

"It's a chance," Judy agreed. "Our only one. We

can get to the ski lift quicker than we can to Weston or to Bledlow Inn by way of the road."

Miss Ward had made up her mind. "We'll try it," she decided. "But only the best skiers. Beverly, you and Betty and Ardeth are to remain here with Kathleen. Whatever happens, don't wander away from the lodge."

"We'll stick close," Ardeth promised.

"I'll go with Virginia and Judy," Miss Ward said. "We'll return as quickly as we can. Don't worry if we're delayed."

Judy and Virginia already were zipping up their heavy jackets. In a twinkling they had adjusted their skis and were off into the gathering twilight.

Going ahead, Judy selected the easier slopes which already were deeply shadowed. Soon they were compelled to climb. They maintained a fast, tiring pace, knowing that every minute counted.

Despite their best efforts, darkness was settling as they finally came within view of the ski lift. Judy, who was in the lead, paused a moment to catch her breath. Her gaze swept the mountainside, noting that the slopes above Bledlow Inn were deserted of skiers. She had hoped desperately that even if the lift no longer carried persons up the mountain, the descending chairs would remain in use. Now she saw no movement whatsoever. The lift had closed for the night.

The Pursuit

"It's no use Miss Ward exclaimed. "We're too late. I was afraid of it."

"We may as well turn back," Virginia said dispiritedly. "We should have gone to Weston where we could have 'phoned."

"We're so close now," Judy replied. "We may as well press on. If the lift has closed, we can ski down."

"It will be too dark," Miss Ward protested. "Night is closing in very fast now."

The trio plunged on at a slower pace, for they had lost heart. But as they struggled the last few yards to the summit of the ridge, Judy suddenly cried that she could see a light burning in the little shack at the top of the lift.

"Someone still may be there!" she exclaimed.

Breathless from exertion, the three reached the little house. The same youthful attendant to whom Judy had spoken on a previous occasion, was preparing to lock up for the night. He stared incredulously at the three.

"Where did you folks come from?" he demanded. "The lift's closed."

"Please start it again," Judy pleaded. "We must get down to the inn."

"Sorry, regulations."

"It's vitally important," Miss Ward urged. She tried to explain the need for haste, but even to her own ears it sounded overly dramatic, almost melodramatic, to say that they were trying to head off a criminal.

"Who are you trying to stop?" the attendant asked doubtfully.

"We don't know his name," Miss Ward confessed. "Not his real one, that is. He's been passing himself off as Caleb Shively at the Scout lodge."

"He's that same man you told me you saw poking about in the ruins of the wrecked transport," Judy contributed. "Oh, please help us!"

"I may get fired for disobeying orders," the attendant returned. "I'll do it though! Get into the chairs, and fasten yourselves in."

With alacrity they obeyed. There was a little delay and then the lift began to operate. The trio descended fast, passing an endless chain of empty chairs which moved up the mountain.

At the little house below, Miss Ward and her two charges slid out onto a long wooden platform. Another attendant met them, demanding to know why they had broken the regulations.

"What gives?" he threw at them. "You folks figure you're privileged characters?"

"This is an emergency," Miss Ward replied tersely. "We'll explain later. No time now."

The three had removed their skis while on the lift. Abandoning their equipment at the little house, they raced for Bledlow Inn across the road adjoining the parking lot.

The Pursuit

"Shively was to meet someone here," Judy murmured, scanning the long row of parked cars. "If only we know who it was!"

"What time is it?" Virginia gasped, hard pressed to keep up with the other two.

"Ten after seven," Miss Ward informed with a quick glance at her wristwatch.

"And the appointment was at seven sharp," Judy said. "Oh, dear!"

"Unless Shively caught a ride to the inn, we may not be too late," the teacher said, retaining hope.

They struggled over the frozen, rutty road to the lighted building. Inside the rustic chalet all was good cheer, with a crackling log and a roomful of gay, laughing young people enjoying hot drinks. Hamburgers and hot dogs were being served from a big stove with a bright copper hood.

Heads turned as the three came in, for there was about them an air of urgency that alerted the entire room. A number of skiers, fearing that there might have been an accident on the mountain, pushed back their coffee cups, and half rose from their chairs.

Judy and Miss Ward anxiously scanned the faces. The one for whom they searched was not there.

"Looking for someone?" inquired the proprietor.

Miss Ward nodded and described the man for whom they searched.

"He was here a few minutes ago," the proprietor

recalled. "He met a man who drove up in a rented car. They went away together."

"Which direction?"

"West, I think. I didn't pay too much attention."

"How can I get in touch with state highway patrol headquarters?" Miss Ward asked tersely.

"We have a phone you may use." The proprietor showed his surprise at the question. "This way, please."

He directed Miss Ward to a private telephone booth. Judy and Virginia waited outside until she had finished the conversation.

"There, I've done everything I can," Miss Ward said, when presently she emerged from the booth. "I've asked the highway department to put out an alarm. If Shively and his friend are anywhere in this area, they should be picked up."

"What's our move now?" Virginia asked, leaning wearily against the wall.

"We'll have to get back to the lodge as fast as we can. I don't want the girls there alone at night. This time, though, we ride. I'll engage a taxi."

While Miss Ward was making arrangements for transportation, Judy and Virginia went back into the grill room. They ordered three cups of hot chocolate and waited for their leader to join them.

As they sat there, tired and rather dejected, a stir of excitement went over the room. The two girls looked quickly around, unaware of anything unusual.

The Pursuit

"Some word must have come over the short wave radio," Judy said, observing that a group of skiers had gathered at the lunch counter near the instrument. "I wonder what—"

Her words were broken by the shrill scream of a siren. An ambulance limousine, its red light flashing a warning, roared past the inn to be lost in the darkness of the highway.

Chapter 24

Emergency Alarm

THOSE in the inn were not long in doubt as to the cause of the ambulance run. From the shortwave radio they learned that a car had skidded off the icy road three miles distant, and that two men, the driver and a passenger had been trapped in the wreckage.

"Wouldn't be surprised if it's that pair you're looking for," the proprietor told Miss Ward. "They were hitting it up when they left here."

A number of men at the inn had decided to drive to the scene of the accident. Miss Ward, Judy and Virginia received an invitation to ride along, and accepted it.

When their car reached the accident scene, it was stopped by a highway patrolman, who temporarily held traffic at a standstill. The highway ahead was blocked by the ambulance and highway cars.

As the girls scrambled out onto the icy road, they saw an automobile, a twisted mass of steel, lying on its side in a ditch beyond the broken guardrail. Only a miracle, it seemed, had saved the car from rolling on down the mountainside.

"It must have gone around the curve too fast," Virginia said with a shudder. "Those poor men! Are they dead?"

Emergency Alarm

A circle of men opened up ahead to permit stretcher bearers to carry two blanket-covered figures toward the ambulance. Judy pushed forward into the arc of light created by the electric lanterns.

"Anyone know these motorists?" inquired a state patrolman. "They were using a rented car."

Judy stared down at one of the dark, bruised faces. The man was fully conscious, though obviously in pain. He stared back at her with insolent recognition.

"You!" he muttered. "I might have known it!"

"You're acquainted with this man, Miss?" the patrolman asked. "Can you tell us his name?"

"He's Caleb Shively. I—I mean he's a fellow who impersonated him," Judy corrected herself.

"This must be the man we were notified to stop for questioning."

"It is," supplied Miss Ward, who had joined the group. "I intend to swear out an arrest warrant."

"Your name?"

"I'm Miss Ward, a Girl Scout leader."

"That's good enough for me," the patrolman nodded. "Do you know this other man too? Apparently he was the driver of the car."

"We don't know his name, but he was on our bus when we came to Weston," Judy informed the patrolman. "I suspect he was helping this other man get away."

"What's the charge against them?"

203

"I'm not sure," Miss Ward replied, somewhat in embarrassment. "The one who calls himself Mr. Shively, took a cigarette case from Judy, and after overpowering Virginia, locked both girls in a bedroom at Maple Leaf Lodge."

"That's larceny, and assault and battery at the least. How valuable is the cigarette case?"

"We don't know," Judy answered. "That's the point. Why would Mr. Shively—this man, I mean, want it at all? It's just a rusty case I picked up at the place where the plane was wrecked."

"Judy thinks the man may be a passenger who escaped at the time of the crash," Miss Ward added.

Already the patrolman was searching the pockets of the man on the stretcher. He produced a few miscellaneous items, and then the missing cigarette case.

"This it?" he demanded.

"Oh, yes!" Judy cried, relieved that it had been found.

The patrolman pocketed the item. "We'll keep it as evidence," he said. "This may be a case for the FBI."

Meanwhile, another patrolman had searched the other injured man, finding papers in his pocket which identified him as Patrick Amboy of New York City. The name at that moment had no significance, but an automatic taken from his overcoat pocket, convinced the officers that they were dealing with criminals. Both men were given first aid treatment, but no attempt was made to question them.

"Are they badly hurt?" Miss Ward asked as the stretchers were shoved into the waiting ambulance.

"The driver of the car is cut up some and has a broken leg," a patrolman told her. "But they both should come through all right."

Under close guard, the ambulance pulled away. Miss Ward was informed that the two men were being taken to a hospital at Bradley, ten miles distant.

The Scout leader was requested to sign a warrant for the arrest of the man who had masqueraded as Mr. Shively, which she willingly agreed to do. The officers themselves placed a technical charge of reckless driving against Mr. Amboy.

"That will hold 'em until the FBI has had a chance to investigate," the patrolman said. "Now, what's all this about Caleb Shively—the real Caleb—being missing?"

Judy, Virginia and Miss Ward related their many unpleasant experiences with the man who had pretended to be caretaker at Maple Leaf Lodge.

"I'm certain he isn't the true caretaker," Judy insisted, "because my brother mailed me a picture of Mr. Shively. He's a much older man."

"That fellow we arrested isn't Shively," the patrolman confirmed. "One of our boys knows Shively quite well."

"We're deeply worried about him," Miss Ward said. "Do you think he might have—"

"I'm afraid of it, Miss," the patrolman cut in, reading her thought. "We're dealing with dangerous criminals. If Mr. X, as I'll call him, is the man I think he may be, he's a wanted spy. Without a means of getting out of this area, he may have hidden himself at the lodge until he could get word to a crony."

"Besides, there must have been something in that plane wreckage that he wanted," added Judy. "That cigarette case likely enough."

"But where is the real Mr. Shively?" Miss Ward asked, reverting to her first worrisome thought. "Weeks now have elapsed since the transport crashed near Penguin Pass."

"I'll round up sheriff's deputies and go with you to the lodge," the patrolman offered. "We'll search the place from top to bottom. I hope Shively is found alive, but I'm not counting on it much."

It was fully an hour later before the party, consisting of four deputies, an assistant sheriff and two patrolmen, finally returned to Maple Leaf Lodge. Miss Ward was relieved to learn that nothing had gone amiss there since her departure. However, the girls who had remained behind had been exceedingly worried over the long absence of the other three.

Judy already had told the officers everything she knew about the habits of Mr. Shively's impersonator, including his irritability whenever anyone tried to enter the locked barn.

"A locked barn eh?" the patrolman inquired. "That's where we'll start our search."

Presently they were all at the door of the barn, waiting tensely as a deputy broke open the heavy padlock. He smashed it and they went in. Mollie, the horse, shivering from cold, whimpered piteously.

"Oh, the poor thing!" Ardeth exclaimed, rushing to the stall. "Not even an ear of corn to eat!"

She and Beverly found a blanket to throw over the animal, and were searching for corn, when they heard an excited shout from the haymow. Two agile deputies had scaled the ladder to investigate the dark hole above.

"We've found Shively!" they called down to the anxious group below. "He's in a bad way, but conscious!"

The deputies would not permit any of the Scouts in the loft. They released the elderly man from the ropes which held him so cruelly fast, and removed a tape which sealed his lips.

Mr. Shively could not walk or stand alone. Carefully he was lowered to the barn floor and carried to the lodge where a bed hastily had been made ready for him. Deputies did all they could for the man's immediate comfort, and then drove to Weston for a doctor.

Meanwhile, warmth and hot soup slowly revived

Mr. Shively. He ran a hand weakly over his unshaven face and grinned.

"Girl Scouts?" he whispered. "Knew you'd come."

"Don't try to talk now," Judy advised. "Later, when you're stronger, we'll tell you everything, and hear your story too."

Both stories had to wait until the following day. By that time, Mr. Shively was able to sit up and take considerable nourishment.

Haltingly, he related to Miss Ward and the girls how misfortune had overtaken him.

"'Twas on the night of the crash," he disclosed. "The Boy Scouts were still here then. I thought I saw a face at the window. I know now that the one who peered in was that villain—his real name's Albert Aldenstein. He must have hid out in the barn for a few days until the Scouts left, and he knew I was alone. Then, spurred on by hunger, he attacked and overpowered me."

"Surely you weren't kept in the barn all those weeks?" Betty gasped. " I should have thought your feet would have been frozen."

"At first Aldenstein held me a prisoner in the lodge. He treated me fairly well before your party came."

"Why did he linger at the lodge?" Judy questioned. "Why didn't he try to get away?"

"I figure it this way. At first everyone was combing the countryside for him. Aldenstein was afraid to

Emergency Alarm

stir. After things quieted down a bit, he decided he wanted to recover a bit of evidence that an FBI man was taking back to Washington."

"A jewelled cigarette case?"

"That might have been it," the caretaker agreed. "Anyway, the evidence involved atomic secrets. Aldenstein had been caught dead to rights, but the matter was being handled quietly—no publicity."

"What happened after our patrol came?" Judy probed. "Were you in the house at the time?"

"I was. I did everything to attract attention, but Aldenstein had me tied up so tight I couldn't do more than thump my feet. No one came."

"You were locked in Aldenstein's room over the kitchen?"

"Right. Then on that first night, he hauled me out by toboggan and kept me in the hayloft. I was able to burrow down into the straw, or I'd have frozen to death these cold nights."

"He fed you though?"

"Yes, and at times he let me exercise enough to restore circulation in my legs."

"No wonder Mr. Aldenstein kept the barn locked and pretended to be so devoted to Mollie," Judy remarked. "As things turned out, I guess it was lucky that Kathleen and I risked that trip to Penguin Pass. It seemed crazy at the time though."

"It's clear enough what happened," said Miss Ward thoughtfully. "Mr. Aldenstein couldn't find the

The Girl Scouts at Penguin Pass

cigarette case in the snow, but you did it for him, Judy. When he learned you had it, he appropriated it and telephoned his accomplice who had come to Weston to help him get out of the country. Then Aldenstein cut the telephone wire and started off to join his friend. Another hour and he'd have been out of the state.

"We were lucky," Virginia declared. "We did our best, but if that car hadn't gone off the road, we might have failed."

Beverly stood near the bedroom window which offered a clear view of the main road.

"Speaking of cars," she drawled, "there's one coming now. More deputies and a state highway patrolman."

"Wonder what's up?" Judy asked eagerly.

"News from the hospital, I think," Miss Ward replied. "One of the deputies sent word earlier today that they're bringing us a first-hand report. Mr. Aldenstein, it seems, has talked, and in doing so, has cleared up a few vital points."

Chapter 25

A Resignation

EXCEPT for Mr. Shively and Kathleen who were confined to their rooms, everyone rushed downstairs to greet the officers. The information they sought so eagerly, immediately was forthcoming.

"Both Aldenstein and Amboy are recovering from their injuries, and are under arrest," one of the deputies told the girls. "They'll be flown to Washington tomorrow."

"Have they confessed?" Ardeth asked.

"Not exactly," the deputy replied with a smile. "We've confirmed most of the facts though. There's no question about identity. It was established this morning by means of fingerprints."

"Did you learn why Aldenstein wanted the cigarette case?"

"The back lid comes off. Inside were hidden some secret formulas. They're of no great value now, but Aldenstein wasn't sure of that. Besides, they were in his handwriting and he must have figured they'd be damaging evidence against him. So he tried to recover the case before he pulled out."

"How did he get in touch with his helper?" Miss Ward questioned.

"That was easy. He put through a telephone call before he snipped the line. After he'd told Amboy to come to Weston and lie low until he was ready to pull out, he holed in here and spent most of his time searching the site of the wreckage. Not at first, of course. He gave the place a wide berth until the community had lost interest."

"If the Scouts hadn't decided to come to Maple Leaf for a week, he might have remained hidden here for months!" Betty commented.

"That's right. You girls tossed a monkey wrench into the machinery. Lucky you did too."

"There's one thing I want to know," declared Judy soberly. "What caused those giant footprints on the trail to Penguin Pass? And was it Aldenstein who built the igloo?"

"Yes, to the latter. After the Scouts descended on him, he was worried lest he might have to pull out fast and have no place to hide until he could join with his friend. So he stocked the ice hut with emergency rations."

"And the huge footprints?"

"Can't you guess?"

"It was some trick—we know that."

"Aldenstein didn't mind explaining about that part," the deputy said. "In fact, it was a dramatic detail of which he seemed rather proud. He made those huge prints to cover his own trail, and also to scare you Scouts away from the Pass.

"But *how*?" demanded Virginia.

A Resignation

"It seems Aldenstein found an old pair of shoes hanging in the barn. A pair that the Boy Scouts had used in a play. So he put them on over his regular ones."

"How dumb we were not to think of that!" Betty chuckled.

"I'd not use that word to describe what you girls have done," the deputy said soberly. "The sheriff asked me to thank you all for your assistance in rounding up those fellows. You've done your country a service."

The Scouts were very happy indeed to receive such praise. Throughout the day, many other people came to the lodge to hear the story of their adventure, to chat with Mr. Shively, and to offer congratulations. By late afternoon the telephone had been repaired once more, the electric lights operated again, and the kitchen was stocked with enough food to last another week.

"Oh, Mr. Hawkins, you shouldn't have brought all those things!" Betty mildly reproved the grocer as he deposited box after box on the kitchen table. "You know our vacation is nearly over now. We'll be leaving in a day or so."

"Don't count on it," Mr. Hawkins grinned.

Betty could obtain no information from him. But a moment later, he delivered to Miss Ward a special message which had been sent by Mr. Medford through the village store. The Girl Scouts were to remain at Maple Leaf Lodge another week, cost free.

"It's little enough to repay the troop for its harrowing experience," the scoutmaster wrote Miss Ward. "We owe your girls a great debt."

As for Mr. Shively, he recovered quickly from his unfortunate captivity. By the following week-end, both he and Kathleen were able to be about again. The girls were delighted to learn that the caretaker was jolly and full of fun, adding a great deal to the merriment.

Making up for lost time, the Scouts skied and tobogganed on the hills near the lodge and frequently went to Bledlow Inn. There, they learned that Amboy and his confederate had been released into the custody of FBI men, who had flown them to Washington.

"Well, that winds up our little adventure," Judy declared one afternoon as the vacation drew near an end. "I never knew so much fun and excitement could be crammed into a few days."

"Nor I," echoed Ardeth, stretching herself like a lazy cat before the crackling log. "Judy, you certainly were given a strenuous introduction to Scouting!"

"And contributed her share to it," added Virginia with a chuckle.

"I've loved every minute of it," Judy declared, her

A Resignation

eyes sparkling. "Everyone has been wonderful to me and cooperative—"

"Everyone?" interposed Beverly Chester in a quiet, almost subdued voice.

She sat by the frosted window, rather alone, staring at her hands which she twisted nervously in her lap. It dawned upon the girls that Beverly had been strangely silent of late.

No one spoke for what reply could be made?

"You all know I've been horrid," Beverly said, speaking hurriedly. "I've been a patrol leader in name only. I didn't live up to many of the Scout laws. I wasn't courteous; I wasn't cheerful, and I'm ashamed to say I wasn't always loyal."

"Hush, Beverly," Kathleen said gently. "Some things are best forgotten. You've changed a lot in the last few days and we're all very fond of you."

"I *have* changed," Beverly went on. "No, don't try to hush me, please. There are things I feel I must say. I'm ashamed of the way I acted toward Judy. Terribly ashamed. I was a bit jealous, I think, of the way she could do everything seemingly without effort. And I was jealous because the girls seemed to like her better than they did me."

"Gracious! I can't do things without effort!" Judy exclaimed. "I'm rash and make many mistakes, such as inducing Miss Ward to let me go to Penguin Pass against her better judgment."

"You're only saying that to make me feel better.

But I'll get to the point. I want to resign as patrol leader."

"Resign?" the girls gasped almost in unison. Beverly's proposal really startled them.

Beverly nodded, fighting back the tears. "Yes, I'm not a natural leader, and I realize it. I want Judy to take over."

"But I'm only a Tenderfoot," Judy protested. "I haven't been a member of the troop long enough. To choose me to lead would be a serious mistake."

"Reconsider," Kathleen urged Beverly. "We really want you and I'm certain you'll do a better job than ever of leading the patrol."

Beverly, however, had made up her mind.

"It's too much of a responsibility and trust," she declared earnestly. "I'm formally handing in my resignation now, and you must select someone to take my place."

"You're not resigning from the troop?" Miss Ward asked quickly.

"Oh, no! I want to be a member of Beaver Patrol always."

"That's better," Miss Ward said in relief. "Well, if you are determined, Beverly, then we'll accept your resignation reluctantly. Later on, you may be induced to take your turn again."

"Perhaps," Beverly smiled.

"I take it nominations are in order," Betty said, glancing toward Judy.

A Resignation

Before anyone could speak her name, Judy made her own proposal. "I nominate Kathleen," she said in a clear, firm voice. "She's steady, dependable, and one of the original members of the patrol. All in favor say 'aye.'"

"Judy!" Kathleen protested with a laugh. "You high-handed little monkey!"

"All in favor say 'aye'," Judy repeated.

"According to good business procedure, one has to close nominations," Kathleen informed the group.

"I move that nominations cease," Virginia contributed. "Those in favor?"

There was a chorus of agreement. Again Kathleen's name was proposed and a unanimous vote was cast for her.

"You're the new patrol leader," Beverly declared well pleased by the election. "Accept my toga and leather-bound copy of the Girl Scout Handbook!"

"I'll do my best to be a good leader," Kathleen said earnestly. "I'll try to live up to your high opinion of me. Now any suggestions or gripes?"

"Just one," grinned Judy. "How much longer must I be known as a Tenderfoot?"

"That depends upon you," supplied Virginia. "You'll be a Second Class Scout as soon as you earn a few badges. Eleven to be exact."

"Where do I start?"

"There are eleven fields of activity from which to choose," Kathleen explained. "For you, the out-of-doors category probably will be the easiest. For instance, a badge may be earned by planning a hike for the troop; where to go, what to wear, what to take."

"She's been doing that ever since she came to Maple Leaf Lodge!" chuckled Betty.

"So I have," Judy agreed, "but the hike that is taking shape now in my brain is a super-duper!"

"Where will we go?" Beverly asked eagerly.

"Can't you guess?"

"Not to Penguin Pass?"

"Only to the trail entrance," Judy responded. She tossed a basketful of chips into the fire and watched the sparks fly up the chimney. "We'll have wonderful food, an outdoor fire, special entertainment—"

"And Monstro, the Snowman as our special guest," drawled Kathleen. "Judy's right, girls. No outing would be complete without him. How could we leave Candy Mountain without saying goodbye to our most faithful and mysterious friend?"